Joy Amid Stress

by Rudolf E. Klimes, PhD

LearnWell Press

for DrugFreeUSA.net

Joy Amid Stress

Published by LearnWell Press for DrugFreeUSA.net
Box 944, Camino CA 95709.

Edited by Anna Homechuk Klimes, EdD
Kathryn Etling, BS
Sue Harmon, BA

All Scripture references are from the *New Living Translation.*
Used by permission of Tyndale House Publishers, Inc.

Library of Congress Cataloging Publication Data
Klimes, Rudolf E.

Joy Amid Stress

Library of Congress Control Number: 2004096024
ISBN 1-886304-11-4

1.   Self-help Techniques, 2. Stress Management
3.   Bible Commentary- Philippians

www.learnwell.org
www.DrugFreeUSA.net
www.klimes.org
www.BibleD.org

edu@learnwell.org
530-644-2123

Printed in the U.S.A. by Morris Publishing,
3212 East Highway 30, Kearney, NE 68847, 1-800-650-7888

Cover Photography Copyright © 1997 by Morris Press

Table of Contents

Part I

Real Joy Amid Stress

1

What About Stress?

Can We Live With it?

It seemed that all happened at once. Tom, just walking through the front door of his home, set off a chain of events that smelled like disaster. Tom's day at work had been hectic; everything that could go wrong had gone wrong. He was exhausted and discouraged. Jill, his oldest daughter, welcomed him in the hall with tears and a bandage around her arm: "I sprained it and now I will not be able to play for a month." In the kitchen, mother barely looked up and handed Tom a bill with the words: "This was due last month. Why didn't you tell me? Where will we ever get the money to pay it now?" Tom said nothing but the 800-pound gorilla of stress had descended on his slumped shoulders to stay awhile.

If you are a parent, grandparent, son, daughter, employee, employer, or retiree, you experience stress.

So many situations can bring on stress that it is impossible to list them. Stress is just there as soon as problems arise. Moreover, there never is a lack of difficulties.

Many people are satisfied with managing or minimizing their stress. But in most cases, the body and mind still knows what is going on and reacts to the pressure, however slight it may be.

Opening up to joy not only roots out stress, but also puts something better in its place. Joy overcomes stress. Joy is the strength that overturns stressful situations.

Stress is a monster that kills millions. It leaves many more troubled and sick. So how can there be joy amid stress? Stress is a harmful reaction to stressful events. Anything that one sees as a problem can produce stress. It does not have to be that way. There are at least three possible reactions to stressful situations.

Destructive Stress is the feeling of anxiety and tension that hurts. Symptoms of destructive stress are, in part, back pain, tiredness, headache, heartburn, high blood pressure, muscle aches, upset stomach, shortness of breath, increased use of cigarettes and alcohol, and weight gain or loss. The most common Destructive Stress is short-term acute stress. Chronic stress often develops from long-term problems such as feeling trapped in a dysfunctional relationship or job.

Managed Stress neutralizes the harmful impact of stressful events. One can learn to cope with stress when trouble rears its ugly head. The pulse will no longer rise; the muscles no longer get tight. This stress is, to a large extent, free from Destructive Stress because people have learned to be strong, healthy and innovative. Most books on stress teach how to manage stress.

Joy Amid Stress is a positive attitude that substitutes something helpful during stressful events. It shifts focus from the overwhelming physical or social problems to spiritual dimensions where joy and gladness rule. It includes Managed Stress that controls the harmful effects of stress. However, it goes beyond that to encourage, easing burdens, to bring things into a positive perspective, to rejoice. In *Joy Amid Stress*, stress is a background noise; joy is the primary player. Thus one can enjoy stressful or peaceful situations nearly alike; in the end, the situation makes little difference. This joy is a supernatural gift that is often not hindered or furthered by stressful or peaceful events.

One classic example of *Joy Amid Stress* is about Paul and Silas sitting in chains in a Philippi dungeon at night, praying and singing aloud. Their joy not only reduced their stress, it trumped it. They counted it joy to be there for the sake of Christ. The difficulty of the situation did not go away, but joy became the lens through which they saw it. Joy became a strength that overshadowed the pain of the situation. Later, locked up in a prison in Rome, Paul could write to the

Philippians (Philippians 2:17) "I want to share my joy with all of you." In this guide we work on reducing stress physically, emotionally and spiritually.

Recently, to empty the compost pail at my daughter's house, I had to go out to the garden on a dark rainy night. Leaving the lighted house behind me, I could see nothing. I did not know where the path was and wandered into the bushes. The darkness was troubling and stressful. Eventually I groped my way to the compost container. After emptying the pail, I turned around and was joyously surprised how the dim lights of the house beautifully defined the path back to the house. Nothing in the garden had changed, but I was no longer walking away from the light, but toward the light. That may illustrate the difference between Destructive Stress and Joy Amid Stress.

Living Amid Stress

Jim, a teenager, had real difficulties with his changing social and physical chemistry. He was often bored, angry and unhappy. He was constantly looking for something that would make him feel great, understood and appreciated. When a friend offered him marijuana, Jim thought he had found his answer to life. Thanks to that drug, he had a calm way about him. It took him quite some time to discover that he was really in trouble. There are better ways to reach joy, a drug-free joy. That is what this guide is all about.

Most people would be happy to get just their stress under control. To be calm amid stress is enough for them. To ask for joy amid stress looks like asking for too much.

Some stress can be minimized by exercise and lifestyle changes. Much emotional and spiritual stress is affected little by these changes and requires a stronger dose of treatment that includes special help. In these cases, reducing stress is not enough. Something needs to be substituted for that stress, and that something is joy.

Stress Kills Joy. Stress eats away at our contentment as well as our stomach linings. It raises blood pressure and hurts our cardiovascular system. It lowers our immune system and contributes to our pains and disabilities. In many cases, it is the single greatest factor that reduces our joy of living and endangers our physical, emotional and spiritual health. It may be that "stress-induced illnesses are the lethal by-products of too much adrenaline pumping through our systems." *The Anxiety Cure* by Archibald D. Hart

Stress Amid Stressful Situations. When all around us things are tied up in trouble and are falling apart, everybody is affected by stress. There is plenty of stress to go around. Stress spreads like a disease and infects everyone.

Joy in Joyful Situations. It is easy to be glad when things go well. Around us there is much support and help for joyous living. The test comes in finding joy when all seems to be against life.

Joy Heals Stress. Joy strengthens the good things in life and smoothes the bumps in the road. By focusing on the positive aspects of life and the blessings that are ours, joy draws on a reservoir of supernatural power to face difficulties courageously. Thus, joy contributes to our ongoing healing.

The purpose of this guide is to help bring inner joy, with all its physical, emotional and spiritual health benefits, into the lives of readers who live in stressful environments.

Physical Health Benefits. The physical health benefits of reducing stress include an active lifestyle that fosters disease prevention and that frees one from unnecessary drug use. Individuals still must avail themselves of medical treatment, procedures and prescribed medication, but in many cases, this book can contribute to the betterment process. The message of Paul's letter to the Philippians, rightly understood and practiced, can contribute positively to the lowering of excessive blood pressure and the healing of stress-related diseases and conditions.

Emotional Health Benefits. Joyous people look at life positively and find a thrill in serving and giving. They do not live mainly for themselves but for others. In doing that, they find a deep satisfaction, that nothing can disturb.

Spiritual Health Benefits. Spiritual health benefits include a way of living that is in harmony with God, that promotes harmonious relationships with others and that gives meaning to our existence.

2

How to Use this Guide

Best Help Groups

Jim gets so much out of his studies as he pours over his books in the quietness of his room. His mind is clear and the thoughts just seem to flow. He finds it thrilling to have the opportunity to learn. But as he joins a neighborhood discussion group, new vistas open up before him. As others share their insights, they trigger other dimensions of thought that are completely new to him. Seeing things from different perspectives, Jim is truly enriched. His neighborhood discussion group is truly his "Best Help Group."

There are at least three ways to relate to God. One is "Alone with God," another is in "**Best** Help Groups" of 6-12 people, and the third is in larger assemblies.

In "**Best**," the "B" stands for "Befriend" (fellowship), the "E" stands for "Eat" (breaking bread, optional), the "S" for "Study" (apostle's doctrine), and the "T" for "Talk with God" (prayers).

The most effective horizontal relationships are covenant commitments to live with others, to become connected with others in a basic Christian community.

Best Help Groups may meet together in homes or restaurants, monthly or twice monthly, with two or more un-churched friends, in Bible study and prayer.

Best Help Groups require commitment: to meet for 3 to 6 months, to study for each session, to support others, to stay on the subject, to keep confidentiality, to enter into deep conversation with God and to help.

1. Befriend in Fellowship: We learn to know the names and phone numbers of group members, we share what we have in common, we care deeply for others regardless of their background, and we grow together in love. We live by I Corinthians 13.

We befriend believers and the un-churched neighbors, friends and relatives and spend time to listen, to help, to share food and joy. Paul wrote:

"[42]They joined with the other believers and devoted themselves to the apostles' teaching and fellowship, sharing in the Lord's Supper and in prayer. [43]A deep sense of awe came over them all, and the apostles performed many miraculous signs and wonders. [44]And all the believers met together constantly and shared everything they had. [45]They sold their possessions and shared the proceeds with those in need. [46]They worshiped together at the Temple each day, met in homes for the Lord's Supper, and shared their meals with great joy and generosity-- [47]all the while praising God and enjoying the goodwill of all the people. And each day the Lord added to their group those who were being saved." Acts 2: 42-47.

2. Eat Together: We break bread together. We share our meals with joy, listen to the inner blessings and pains, and participate in encouraging table talk. The priority is on loving each other.

3. Study Bible Passages: We ask, What does the text mean? What does it mean to me? How do I apply the passage to myself? How can I focus on living the passage? How can I share relevant insight?

Study aids include a Concordance (wordbook), Commentary (for explanations), Bible Dictionary (for definitions), Bible Atlas (for maps) and **www.BibleD.org.**

4. Talk with God: We share in prayer and worship in the Holy Spirit. Every failure is a prayer failure. "The reason you don't have what you want is that you don't ask God for it." James 4:2.

Are you part of a Best Group? Are you involved in doctrine, fellowship, breaking of bread and prayer? If so befriend, eat together, study the Bible, and talk with God.

Consider these five questions: Do you have un-churched friends? Do you want to reach out to them? Do you have time for them? Will you bring them to a group? Do you need to grow in faith?

How To Use This Guide?

1. First, read the beginning unit of this book. That will get you into the subject and you will find out how it all fits together.

2. After that, you are ready to study and prepare for the first set of 13 discussions. Read the pages for the first session and then explore the notes called "Explore it Further." In the notes are comments and insights into the passages that may be helpful in the discussion.

3. Find a discussion group that would like to work with you in the 13 sessions. Or you may organize your own group. Anyone who is willing and able to study stress and the given passages in depth can be considered to lead a group.

4. Go to the Table of Contents and add the dates for your 13 discussions. Also, select a place and time.

5. Discuss the topic of the first session, using this guide. Take your time. Let all participate. Pay special attention to the parts titled *Read and Apply* and *Fit it*. Talking about Joy *amid Stress* is not enough, you have to apply what you learn.

6. After completing the 1st session, plan and implement the 2nd session and so on. As time goes by, you become more familiar with the method used and your benefits will increase.

7. After completing the first set of 13 sessions, go on to the second unit of 13 discussions. After that, consider with your group what topic you would like to study next, using the

Guide for Additional Study at the end of the book. Make the needed arrangements. Or disband the group.

How to Move from Stress to Joy

This volume presents two discussion guides, both in 13 chapters. The following notes are mainly for the second unit, but similar methods may be used for the third unit. One chapter is for each week in a three-month period. Or the studies can be held twice a month over six months. Most groups find that 75-90 minutes is about the right length for each discussion. While designed for group use, this guide may also be used for self-study. Each chapter consists of seven sections. A brief description on how to use each section is here in order. Study each lesson ahead of each meeting. When the group meets, no one should dominate or give unsolicited advice. Anything said should remain confidential. Group members should exchange telephone numbers and stay in contact. The one in charge does not teach but rather facilitates the discussion. Each group member leads out in a part of the discussion.

First Period of 50 Minutes

A. Check the Quotation that Appeals to You the Most. Many authors have commented on the topic under study. Read the two quotations and select the one that appeals to you most. Explain why you like it.

B. Read and Apply. The first nine studies deal with Paul's letter to the Philippians. Each of the four chapters of Philippians is divided into two studies. Read this section very carefully and comment on the issues presented. You may want to use other Bible versions, Bible dictionaries and commentaries to gain a deeper understanding of the text. The last four chapters use other Biblical passages.

Without application, this study guide can be abstract, theoretical and of limited use. Carefully complete the sentences that are presented or at least outline your response. Some sentences call for rather specific personal information that you may be reluctant to share in a group. Do not share what you are not ready to share. Use a notebook for your answers if you find the space provided inadequate.

Second Period of 25 minutes

C. Circle T for True and F for False and Give Reasons. You will find a number of statements in a box, some of them are true and some are false. Read them over and then circle T for True or F for False. More statements are true than false. There is no key to the questions since the answers may depend on your perception of the issue. Suggest the reasons that contributed to your choice.

D. Fit It. This guide does not deal only with spiritual and emotional health, but also physical health. Thus in this section are suggestions for activities you can do to stay fit and free of stress. This section deals with the implementing of the learned concepts. If possible, fit them into your life and report on your progress the next meeting.

Homework or Discussion if there is Time

E. Consider This. Please consider the short case presented here. The last sentence of the case is always a question to which you may want to respond. There may not be a right or wrong answer.

F. Remember. The deeper the lessons go into your mind, the more likely you will apply what you are learning. The short passages in this section are useful for memorization. You may also want to print these statements and place them around the house as reminders. Also, study the next chapter.

G. Journal It. You learn most if you read and review all sections in the chapter under study throughout your week. For this, a joy journal, a stress journal or a prayer journal may be helpful. You may write there your joys, your daily meditations, your prayers, your reactions to what you read and experience, and comments from the Application section. Such a journal is for you alone unless you choose to share it with others.

H. Explore it Further. In this section, you will find further comments and notes about the chapter. The paragraphs are numbered P1, P2, etc so that group members can be called upon to read specific paragraphs.

3

Why Philippians?

Can We Learn From the Ancients?

The main wisdom-source for this guide is Paul's letter to the Philippians. This short ancient text that has stood the test of time is a very encouraging and joy-promoting manuscript. The Apostle Paul discovered joy when in the confines of a Roman prison. He has something to teach us who live in much less stressful circumstances. Now stay with this guide and find your joy.

The first nine discussions of this guide are based on the ancient letter that the Apostle Paul wrote to the people of Philippi. Paul reflects with deep emotions on his joy in regards to the Philippians. The letter serves as the basic text for most of this study. The Bible version used is the New Living Translation. Here is a short introduction to the letter that deals with the basics, as a reporter would ask six basic questions.

WHO: Paul is writing to Christians in Philippi and to us.
Paul founded the Philippi church about AD 50 after God's call by a man from Macedonia. That story is in Acts 16. Among the church members were Lydia, a jailer and Epaphroditus.

The Philippians were citizens of an ancient city in Macedonia called Philippi. Paul visited there and made close friends with some of its residents. He wrote them a letter that is now part of the Bible. In this letter, Paul expresses his joy at the Philippians' calmness in the presence of political and spiritual storms that rage all around them.

WHAT: Spiritual joy and peace may permeate all aspects of life.

This short letter uses the word joy and similar words more than a dozen times. The emphasis is on spiritual joy and contentment even in a Roman city where there was often strife and trouble.

WHEN: About AD 62.
The exact date of this letter is not given. It was probably written between AD 61-64.

WHERE: To the believers in Philippi, likely from Rome.
It seems that Paul was imprisoned in Rome. Philippi was one of Paul's favorite churches. He had a deep attachment to the believers there. Timothy was with him in Rome when Paul wrote this letter.

Philippi was a city in Macedonia in Northeast Greece founded by the father of Alexander the Great in 360 BC to mine gold. It was a Roman colony and was considered a miniature Rome. The believers were mainly Gentiles.

WHY: For encouragement and strength in troubled times.
Trouble brings stress and discomfort to all. Christians have a Savior who can bring joy in the midst of storms. Some Christians experience joy while others do not. It is God's will that people would trust Christ to see them through all difficulties and retain joy in spite of outside pressures.

HOW: God's love and prayers of thanksgiving can bring joy.
This letter is a guide to joyous living. Paul, by inspiration, discusses various circumstances that lead either to stress or to joy. Lack of faith is generally associated with stress, and faith with joy. Because God watches over His people, they have nothing to fear and can experience joy regardless of the stressors.

Trust + Love = Joy. Trusting Christ to guide us, and loving others, results in joy.

In writing this encouraging letter from prison to old friends, Paul showed that he could experience joy in the midst of the storm. Here Paul revealed the secret of his inner peace and joy, namely his faith. The old word for stress is distress. The Bible often links distress with trouble.

4

Do Drugs Really Harm?

Can We live Drug-Free?

Jim and Mary live in a drug-dominated world. So do most of us. As Mary turns on her television for the morning news, she is bombarded with advertising for medications that are supposed to heal whatever is wrong.

After that, she needs something to get going. Her breakfast cup of coffee too is a drug.

Jim's friends at work feel heavily the stress at work. During their coffee break, some go out in the back to have a smoke. Their dose of nicotine too is a drug. Others get their coke from the vending machine. Their dose of caffeine too is a drug.

After work, Jim wants to relax. He goes to the fridge and gets a beer. His dose of alcohol too is a drug.

Jim and Mary do not think that these common and legal drugs can harm them. And in a way they are right, their bodies can take this punishment for a while. But not forever.

Can we live drug-free? Considering the normal use and abuse of the above-mentioned drugs in our culture, the answer is a resounding yes. Most of us can get along well without caffeine, nicotine and alcohol. We further do not need what are called recreational drugs. Drugs are potentially far too harmful to take them for fun.

Then there are over-the-counter medications that are overused. Many people are used to popping pills for whatever ails them. Rather than eating right or drinking plenty of water, they consume pills. Rather than exercising and changing their lifestyle, they take pills.

There seem to be prescription drugs for every problem. Some are very helpful and effective; others bring on side effects that are worse than the problem. Some people take their doctor-prescribed medications regularly and thus can cope with life. Others seem to exist on a diet of 10 or 20 drugs. Sadly, with many diseases, we have little choice but to take the prescribed medications.

Drugs are for medical purposes. But many people treat their stress with drugs. Drugs are seldom the solution to our stress. Many times, drugs are one of the causes of our stress. To take them carelessly, just as a food or drink, harms the body and increases our chances of stress. A large portion of modern diseases is related to the misuse of harmful drugs.

A drug-free life lets you face your problems without chemical manipulation. In the end, caffeine, nicotine, alcohol and the illegal drugs are not helpful, they are harmful. They may give a person a short lift, but eventually, they take their revenge. Young people are often so strong that drugs do not seem to harm them. However, they may contribute to disease. Some harm slowly or contribute bit by bit to the body stress they are supposed to relieve.

Drugs harm in many ways. Many drugs are addictive. Once involved with them, it is hard to stop. Millions use drugs not because they enjoy them or find them helpful, but because they cannot give them up. Often it takes more and more of the drug to receive the same satisfaction.

Many people use drugs they cannot afford. Drug-use is an expensive hobby. Money that could help foster the joy of living is often wasted in polluting the air and brains.

Many drugs mask the real psychological or physical health difficulty and thus interfere with constructive problem solving. People who seek some relief from their daily stress sincerely believe that drugs take their stress away. A few beers do not make marital problems go away. They just delay their solution, often until it is too late.

Drug use is in many ways an emotional problem. Not able to express honestly their emotions, kids and adults cope with the help of drugs. Drugged, they feel able to do what they want to do. Since often they then cannot see the consequences, they feel invincible. After the drug wears off, they are worse off than when they started.

A drug-free lifestyle avoids many of these problems. It frees a person to seek help outside of him or her. Stress can be replaced by joy. Help can take the place of harm.

Staying Drug-Free

Here are some ways for parents to help their children stay drug-free and relieve stress from the US Department of Health and Human Services at www.mentalhealth.org:

The 15+ Make Time to Listen...Take Time to Talk Campaign is based on the premise that parents who talk with their children about what is happening in their lives are better able to guide their children toward more positive, skill-enhancing activities and friendships. The campaign provides practical guidance for parents and caregivers on how to strengthen their relationship with their children by spending at least 15 minutes of daily, undivided time with them and focusing on them.

It really can make a difference when you get involved in your child's life. Young people are much less likely to have mental health and substance use problems when they have positive activities to do and when caring adults are involved in their lives. Your involvement and encouragement tell your child that he or she and his activities are worthwhile and may help him identify and pursue positive goals as he gets older. Additionally, you will be better able to see changes in your child that may indicate a problem.

Make clear, sensible rules for your child and enforce them with consistency and appropriate consequences. When you do this, you help your child develop daily habits of self-discipline. Following these rules can help protect your child's physical safety and mental well-being, which can lower her risk for substance abuse problems.

Some rules, such as "Respect Your Elders," apply to all ages, but many will vary depending on your child's age and level of development.

Set a good example for your child. Think about what you say and how you act at all times. Your child learns social skills and ways to deal with stress by listening to you and watching you. Do not take part in illegal, unhealthy, or dangerous practices related to alcohol, tobacco, or illegal drugs or he may believe that, no matter what you say, these practices are acceptable.

Support your child's social development. Teach your child how to form positive relationships. Research shows that the pressure to use tobacco, alcohol, and illegal drugs comes most often from wanting to be accepted, wanting to belong, and wanting to be noticed. Help your child learn what qualities to look for in a friend, and advise him about what to say if offered harmful substances. Children who have difficulty making friends need your support to avoid being isolated or bullied.

Do you know what your child listens to and reads and how she spends time with her friends? Talking with your child about her interests opens up an opportunity for you to share your values. And research says that monitoring your child's activities is an important way to lower her chances of getting involved in situations you don't approve of, especially those that can be harmful. Unsupervised children simply have more opportunities to experiment with risky behaviors, including the use of alcohol, tobacco, and illegal drugs, and they may start substance abuse at earlier ages.

This unit introduced *Joy Amid Stress*. The discussions that follow are to be used by groups or individuals. Select dates for the various studies and start your journey into joy now.

Part II

Discussion Guide for

Experiencing
Joy Amid Stress

1

Joy in Isolation

Paul and The Philippians

You cannot easily escape the stress that comes from living in this world. However, you can find joy in living for a larger purpose. Joyously bloom wherever you are planted. (Define joy.)

A. Check the Quotation that Appeals to You the Most

__ "This communicating of a man's self to his friend works two contrary effects, for it redoubles joys, and cuts grief in half." Francis Bacon, *Essays*

__ "There are souls in this world which have the gift of finding joy everywhere and of leaving it behind them when they go." Frederick Faber

B. Read and Apply the Wisdom about Joy in Paul's Letter to the Philippians from a Roman Prison, AD 61-64

All applications deal with you, so be honest as you respond to some rather personal matters. You can write in the answers here in outline form in the blanks or you may write longer explanations in a notebook. In the group, one person responds to the first blank, another to the second question, and so on.

Philippians 1:1, 2 "This letter is from Paul and Timothy, slaves of Christ Jesus. It is written to all of God's people in Philippi, who believe in Christ Jesus, and to the elders and deacons."

Q1:1, 2. This letter is to all God's people, including (tell who you are). The letter "Q" stands for "Question."

_____.

[1:4] "I always pray for you, and I make my requests with a heart full of joy."

Q1:4. I always pray for _____.

Q1:4. I have a heart full of joy when I_____.

[1:18] "But whether or not their motives are pure, the fact remains that the message about Christ is being preached, so I rejoice. And I will continue to rejoice."

Q1:18. I rejoice. I will continue to rejoice even when

_____.

[1:25] "I am convinced of this, so I will continue with you so that you will grow and experience the joy of your faith."

Q1:25. I grow and experience the joy of my faith when I

_____.

[2:2] "Make me truly happy by agreeing wholeheartedly with each other..."

Q2.2. Others makes me truly happy by

_____.

[2:17, 8] "But even if my life is to be poured out like a drink offering to complete the sacrifice of your faithful service (that is, if I am to die for you), I will rejoice, and I want to share my joy with all of you. And you should be happy about this and rejoice with me."

Q2:17, 18. I will rejoice, and I want to share my joy

especially with _____.

2:28,29 "You will be glad to see him [Epaphroditus], and that will lighten all my cares. Welcome him with Christian love and with great joy, and be sure to honor people like him."

Q2:28, 29. I usually welcome with Christian love and with

great joy _____.

3:1 "Whatever happens, dear brothers and sisters, may the Lord give you joy. I never get tired of telling you this. I am doing this for your own good."

Q3:1. May the Lord give me joy when I

_____.

4:1 "Dear brothers and sisters, I love you and long to see you, for you are my joy and the reward for my work. So please stay true to the Lord, my dear friends."

Q4:1. My joy and reward for my work is

_____.

4:4 "Always be full of joy in the Lord. I say it again--rejoice!"

Q4:4. I am always full of joy when I

_____.

You will find these passages also in later chapters. They are brought together here to show Paul's joy even while imprisoned in Rome.

C. Circle T for True or F for False and Give Reasons
- T F The Bible Way is the way of peace that avoids all hurts.
- T F Coming into spiritual & social harmony brings joy.
- T F Growth in faith results in the fruits of peace and joy.

D. Fit It

Experience the stress-reducing joy of your faith (Philippians 1:25) by:
- Walking or exercising daily for at least 30 minutes.
- Eating three healthy sit-down meals daily that exclude junk food.
- Limiting or eliminating all unnecessary drugs like alcohol, tobacco, and caffeine.
- Thinking positively and reviewing your many blessings.
- Keeping your prayer life steady.

F. Remember It: We are in trouble, but not crushed or broken (Paraphrased 2 Cor 4:8). We are too blessed to be stressed.

G. Journal It: See notes concerning journaling on pages 14 and 125.

H. Explore it Further

P1. Hebrews 10:34
You suffered along with those who were thrown into jail. When all you owned was taken from you, you accepted it with joy. You knew you had better things waiting for you in eternity.

P2. Hebrews 12:2
We do this by keeping our eyes on Jesus, on whom our faith depends from start to finish. He was willing to die a shameful death on the cross because of the joy he knew would be his afterward. Now he is seated in the place of highest honor beside God's throne in heaven.

2

The Joy of Thanking

***

Philippians 1:2-11

***

You cannot easily change the world around you to fit your needs. But you can thank God for His many blessings. You have so much for which you can be joyously thankful.

A. Check the Quotation that Appeals to You the Most

__ "Be thankful for problems. If they were less difficult, someone with less ability might have your job." Bits & Pieces

__ "Trouble is here. It is for a purpose. Use it for the purpose for which it was intended--to help you grow. Thank God for your troubles." Dr. Norman Vincent Peale

B. Read and Apply the Wisdom of Thanksgiving and Prayer

[1:2] May God our Father and the Lord Jesus Christ give you grace and peace.

Q2 Christ gives me peace in

_____.

[3]Every time I think of you, I give thanks to my God. [4]I always pray for you, and I make my requests with a heart full of joy [5]because you

have been my partners in spreading the Good News about Christ from the time you first heard it until now. [6]And I am sure that God, who began the good work within you, will continue his work until it is finally finished on that day when Christ Jesus comes back again.

Q3. I give thanks to my God especially for

_____.

Q4. I always pray for

_____.

Q4-5 My heart is full of joy because

_____are my partners in spreading the Good News.

[7]It is right that I should feel as I do about all of you, for you have a very special place in my heart. We have shared together the blessings of God, both when I was in prison and when I was out, defending the truth and telling others the Good News. [8]God knows how much I love you and long for you with the tender compassion of Christ Jesus.

Q8. I have the tender compassion of Christ Jesus toward

_____.

[9]I pray that your love for each other will overflow more and more, and that you will keep on growing in your knowledge and understanding. [10]For I want you to understand what really matters, so that you may live pure and blameless lives until Christ returns.

Q9. I keep on growing in knowledge and understanding by

_____.

Q10. What really matters in my life is

_____.

¹¹"May you always be filled with the fruit of your salvation--those good things that are produced in your life by Jesus Christ--for this will bring much glory and praise to God."

Q11. The good things that are produced in my life by Jesus Christ are

_____.

C. Circle T for True or F for False and Give Reasons
- T F Peace is the result of living without stress, by the power of God's freely given love.
- T F Joy is inner peace in times of success, failure, pressures and hardships.
- T F The Fruits of Salvation are grown by Christ in those who stay connected to Him.

D. Fit It

Pray, meditate and make your requests with a heart full of joy (1:4)
- Select a peaceful place and breathe in slowly on "1" and exhale slowly on "1, 2, 3." Do it 10 times.
- Lift your arms up and breathe in, put your arms down and breathe out. Up-in, down-out.
- Choose a Bible verse, repeat it, visualize it, and let it soak in.
- Let go and relax every body part completely, from your toes to your scalp.
- Thank people around you for their kindness.

E. Consider This

Jane has recently accepted Jesus as her Savior. She realizes that her newfound joy is a gift from God. Her spiritual life has started to enrich her with peace. Her prayers are songs of thanks. But her physical life is in turmoil as she tries so hard to do all that she feels Christ expects of her. How can she become satisfied with God's blessings without feeling stressed?

F. Remember: **May your love overflow and keep on growing** (Paraphrased Philippians 1:9).

G. Journal It

H. Explore it further

"I always pray for you, and I make my requests with **a heart full of joy**." Phil 1:4

P1. Praying for someone who is dear to your heart is a joy. Just thinking about that person brings joy. The privilege to take that person into the presence of God is indeed a joyous event. Praying anytime is a joy, but sharing that prayer with a loved one makes it a double joy. Paul's physical circumstances in prison were a constant hardship to him, but his prayers and recollections of friends were islands of joy.

P2. It is a real pleasure to think and pray about a good friend. That was Paul's case with the Philippians. Paul would have special sessions of prayers for his friends by name, and that included the Philippians. Even so he had been mistreated there in prison, he remembered happily the kindness of the local Christians.

P3. "Much of Paul's joy was based on the pleasant, loving recollections of believers who, like those in Philippi, were constantly

29

faithful to the Lord, to their fellow believers, and to him" (John MacArthur, Jr., p 20)

P4. Paul was able to ignore to some extent his own circumstances and focus on the wonderful Philippi believers. Paul did not focus on his own difficult position and lament his condition. He lived above that. His life was so connected with his Lord and serving his fellow men that he could ignore his own hardships. He was not the center of his ministry, but the Lord was. The Lord gave him joy amid the stress of imprisonment. One of the reasons for Paul's joy was his partnership with the Philippians in the work of the gospel. They had served together as missionaries. They had helped each other, and out of that working relationship came a great respect for one another. It was not that Paul was the preacher and great apostle and that the Philippians were just listeners. They all worked together for the same Lord. Paul was very respectful of the believers, and the believers were most considerate of Paul and his needs.

P5. "Lack of joy reveals itself in three ways: in negative thoughts and talks about others, in a lack of concern for their welfare, and in the failure to intercede on their behalf. Joyless believers are self-centered, selfish, proud, and often vengeful, and their self-centeredness inevitably manifests itself in prayerlessness." (MacArthur, p 22)

P6. *"Love* and *joy* are the two first-fruits of the Spirit. *Joy* gives especial animation to prayers. It marked his [Paul's] high opinion of them [Philippians], that there was almost everything in them to give him *joy,* and almost nothing to give him pain." (Jamieson)

3

The Joy of Trusting

You cannot trust everyone. But you can find and enjoy relationships that are truly trustworthy. What joy to lean on someone who will not let you down!

A. Check the Quotation that Appeals to You the Most

__ "Courage, brother! do not stumble, / Though thy path be dark as night; / There's a star to guide the humble: / `Trust in God, and do the right'." Norman Macleod, Hymn: "Trust in God"

__ "There is nothing in life so difficult that it cannot be overcome. This faith can move mountains. It can change people. It can change the world. You can survive all the great storms in your life." Dr. Norman Vincent Peale

B. Read and Apply the Privilege of Trusting.

[12] And I want you to know, dear brothers and sisters, that everything that has happened to me here has helped to spread the Good News. [13] For everyone here, including all the soldiers in the palace guard, knows that I am in chains because of Christ. [14] And because of my imprisonment, many of the Christians here have gained confidence and become more bold in telling others about Christ.

Q12. Everything that happened to me has helped

_____.

Q14. Many of the Christians here have gained confidence

because I _____.

[15]Some are preaching out of jealousy and rivalry. But others preach about Christ with pure motives. [16]They preach because they love me, for they know the Lord brought me here to defend the Good News. [17]Those others do not have pure motives as they preach about Christ. They preach with selfish ambition, not sincerely, intending to make my chains more painful to me.

Q16. The Lord brought me here to

_____.

[18]But whether or not their motives are pure, the fact remains that the message about Christ is being preached, so I rejoice. And I will continue to rejoice. [19]For I know that as you pray for me and as the Spirit of Jesus Christ helps me, this will all turn out for my deliverance.

Q18. I will continue to rejoice especially when

_____.

[20]For I live in eager expectation and hope that I will never do anything that causes me shame, but that I will always be bold for Christ, as I have been in the past, and that my life will always honor Christ, whether I live or I die. [21]For to me, living is for Christ, and dying is even better. [22]Yet if I live, that means fruitful service for Christ. I really don't know which is better. [23]I'm torn between two desires: Sometimes I want to live, and sometimes I long to go and be with Christ. That would be far better for me, [24]but it is better for you that I live.

Q20. My life will always honor Christ by

_____.

²⁵I am convinced of this, so I will continue with you so that you will grow and experience the joy of your faith. ²⁶Then when I return to you, you will have even more reason to boast about what Christ Jesus has done for me.

Q25. I grow and experience the joy of my faith by

_____.

²⁷But whatever happens to me, you must live in a manner worthy of the Good News about Christ, as citizens of heaven. Then, whether I come and see you again or only hear about you, I will know that you are standing side by side, fighting together for the Good News. ²⁸Don't be intimidated by your enemies. This will be a sign to them that they are going to be destroyed, but that you are going to be saved, even by God himself. ²⁹For you have been given not only the privilege of trusting in Christ but also the privilege of suffering for him. ³⁰We are in this fight together. You have seen me suffer for him in the past, and you know that I am still in the midst of this great struggle.

Q27. I live in a manner worthy of the Good News in

_____.

Q29. For me, the privilege of suffering for Christ means to

_____.

C. Circle T for True or F for False and Give Reasons

- T F Difficulties and tests may be faced without undue stress as part of character development.
- T F In God's peace, nothing can terrify us.
- T F The central joy that Christians experience is the joy of faith, service and being loved.

D. Fit It

My spiritual and physical life will always honor Christ (1:20) by the way:
- I study and share God's word.
- I treat others.
- I keep myself physically fit.
- I discipline my eating.
- I use prayer and meditation.
- I trust trustworthy friends.

E. Remember: "My life will always honor Christ, whether I live or die" (Philippians 1:20).

G. Journal It

H. Explore it further

"But whether or not their motives are pure, the fact remains that the message about Christ is being preached, so **I rejoice. And I will continue to rejoice.**" Phil 1:18

P1. One of Paul's problems in the prison in Rome was the work of some fellow Christians with selfish motives. It must have caused him considerable stress to hear about strange preachers when he himself was not free to go out and correct them. A lesser man would have been very troubled and possibly discouraged by it. Not so Paul.

P2. "Their *chief* error was their self-seeking envious *motive,* not so much error of doctrine; had there been *vital* error, Paul would not have *rejoiced.* The *proclamation of* CHRIST," however done, roused attention, and so was sure to be of service. Paul could thus rejoice at the good result of their bad intentions." (Jamieson)

P3. Paul left the evaluation of motives to God. He did not feel that it was his job to see to it that the motives of all his fellow-workers were correct. Anyway, only God can read the heart and motives. So why make an issue of it? Paul was concerned about motives, for he writes about it. Then he ends this section by focusing on the outcome, namely that the gospel was being preached. To him that was the important thing. And a source of rejoicing and joy.

P4. Paul sees his situation not from his own limitations in prison, which included discomforts, restrictions and anxiety. He saw life around him from the perspective of God. Because he was in prison, the gospel was being preached in various ways in places to which it would never have reached. That was Paul's life, his constant joy. Nothing could limit that joy which was God's personal gift to him.

P5. "Absolutely nothing could steal Paul's God-given joy. He was expendable; the gospel was not. His own privacy and freedom were incidental and he cared nothing for personal recognition or credit.... Paul's example of selfless humility shows that the worse the circumstances are, the greater joy can be." (MacArthur, p 69)

P6. "The preaching of Christ is the joy of all who wish well to his kingdom among men. Since it may tend to the good of many, we ought to rejoice in it, though it is done in pretence, and not in reality. It is God's prerogative to judge of the principles men act upon; this is out of our line. Paul was so far from envying those who had liberty to preach the gospel while he was under confinement that he rejoiced in the preaching of it even by those who do it in pretence, and not in truth. How much more then should we rejoice in the preaching of the gospel by those who do it in truth, yea, though it should be with much weakness and some mistake!" (Matthew Henry)

> "I am convinced of this, so I will continue with you so that you will grow and experience **the joy of your faith.**" Phil 1:25

P7. The joy of faith does not come easily; it comes as a gift of the Spirit to growing Christians. Without that growth, there may be faith, but no joy of faith. Thus, it is easy to tell a growing Christian by the measure of his or her joy. A dried-up Christian has no faith or joy to share. Joy must flow as a fresh stream from the heart of God; it cannot be kept in a cup for future use.

P8. "What promotes our *faith and joy of faith* is very much for our furtherance in the way to heaven. The more faith the more joy, and the more faith and joy the more we are furthered in our Christian course. There is need of a settled ministry, not only for the conviction and conversion of sinners, but for the edification of saints, and their furtherance in spiritual attainments." (Matthew Henry)

P9. The growth in faith and the experience of joy in faith are connected. Without growth in faith, there is no joy in faith. The Christian cannot rest on his faith without growing it. The growth may be slow or fast, but there has to be a constant development of one's faith. If your faith today is the same as it was a year ago, it is most likely a faith without the exuberant joy that is God's gift to growing Christians.

P10. It is not just a matter of having joy, but Paul wants us to experience it. God wants us to apply it in the various circumstances of our lives. Faith is in itself a joyous experience because it links us to the source of all Power. With faith in a risen Savior, the gloom of the tomb is lifted and the joy of heaven has become a daily reality. That joy is then inside us, around us, behind us and wherever we turn. The pain is gone. Joy has taken over.

P11. Joy in many ways is a foretaste of heaven. Where on this earth we live with joy amid pain and stress, in the atmosphere of heaven only the joy remains. There will be no more sorrow, no more tears, and no more impossible deadlines. Thus experiencing the joy of faith is to drink of the joy of heaven. God grants a foretaste of the joy of heaven to those who keep growing in faith.

"The joy of Christ is a pure, unalloyed cheerfulness. It is not a cheap gaiety that leads to vanity of words or lightness of conduct. No, we are to have His joy, and His greatest joy was to see men obeying the truth." (White, 293)

4

The Joy of Befriending

You cannot easily befriend everybody. But you can enjoy life with friends who share your life mission and will let you in. Your friends are there for you by your side when you really need them.

A. Check the Quotation that Appeals to You the Most

__ "There are only two people who can tell you the truth about yourself--an enemy who has lost his temper and a friend who loves you dearly." Antisthenes

__ "Don't walk behind me, I may not lead. Don't walk in front of me, I may not follow. Just walk beside me and be my friend." Albert Camus

B. Read and Apply Unity through Humility

[1]Is there any encouragement from belonging to Christ? Any comfort from his love? Any fellowship together in the Spirit? Are your hearts tender and sympathetic? [2]Then make me truly happy by agreeing wholeheartedly with each other, loving one another, and working together with one heart and purpose.

Q1. With whom do you have fellowship in the Spirit?

_____.

Q2. I have to learn to agree wholeheartedly with

_____.

[3]Don't be selfish; don't live to make a good impression on others. Be humble, thinking of others as better than yourself. [4]Don't think only about your own affairs, but be interested in others, too, and what they are doing.

Q3. I live to make a good impression on

_____.

Q4. I am interested in others, especially

_____.

[5]Your attitude should be the same that Christ Jesus had. [6]Though he was God, he did not demand and cling to his rights as God. [7]He made himself nothing; he took the humble position of a slave and appeared in human form. [8]And in human form he obediently humbled himself even further by dying a criminal's death on a cross. [9]Because of this, God raised him up to the heights of heaven and gave him a name that is above every other name, [10]so that at the name of Jesus every knee will bow, in heaven and on earth and under the earth, [11]and every tongue will confess that Jesus Christ is Lord, to the glory of God the Father.

Q5. My attitude is the same that Christ Jesus had when I

_____.

[12]Dearest friends, you were always so careful to follow my instructions when I was with you. And now that I am away you must be even more careful to put into action God's saving work in your lives, obeying God with deep reverence and fear. [13]For God is

working in you, giving you the desire to obey him and the power to do what pleases him.

Q13. God is giving me the power to do what pleases Him, especially _____.

[14]In everything you do, stay away from complaining and arguing, [15]so that no one can speak a word of blame against you. You are to live clean, innocent lives as children of God in a dark world full of crooked and perverse people. Let your lives shine brightly before them. [16]Hold tightly to the word of life, so that when Christ returns, I will be proud that I did not lose the race and that my work was not useless. [17]But even if my life is to be poured out like a drink offering to complete the sacrifice of your faithful service (that is, if I am to die for you), I will rejoice, and I want to share my joy with all of you. [18]And you should be happy about this and rejoice with me.

Q14. I stay away from complaining and arguing best when I

_____.

Q17. I want to share my joy with

_____.

C. Circle T for True or F for False and Give Reasons
- T F Spiritual growth is a joint effort between an individual and the Holy Spirit.
- T F We mind our own business and tactfully help those in need.
- T F As children in God's kindergarten, we keep on growing without stress.

F. Fit It

I work together with my friends with one heart and purpose (v2) to enjoy:
- A walking or exercise group.
- Social activities.
- Eating together.
- Simplicity of living.
- Problem solving, one little thing at a time.

E. Consider That

Jane looked around among her friends and thanked God that she does not have the problems of others. But the better she learned to know some of her friends, the more she found that many of them had strengths she never imagined. How can Jane share in the victories of her friends?

F. Remember: Work "together with one heart and purpose" (Philippians 2:2).

J. Journal It

H. Explore it further

> "**Make me truly happy** by agreeing wholeheartedly with each other..." Phil 2:2

P1. Unresolved differences are a source of pain and stress, wholehearted agreement the soil of joy and happiness. Good friends work out their differences. In the family, in the brotherhood and sisterhood, respectful voluntary agreement makes for a happy working atmosphere.

P2. It takes love, time and effort to reach agreement with others. The biggest obstacles to wholehearted agreement are often a lack of communication and a desire to control by one or both parties. It is not just a matter of submission of one party to the other. That is usually not wholehearted agreement, but a forced agreement that makes nobody happy. Wholehearted agreement requires two hearts that beat like one, that feel for each other. Both parties adjust to each other out of respect and love.

P3. The agreement needs to be not only of the mind but also of the heart, and of feelings. Voting for a project may be easy, but to find wholehearted support and commitment often takes much more persuasion. We are often pushy; satisfied with mental agreement that lacks emotional depth. If something does not feel right, sooner or later these painful feelings will surface to sabotage the mental agreement.

P4. "We are of a like mind when we have the same love. Christians should be one in affection, whether they can be one in apprehension or not. This is always in their power, and always their duty, and is the likeliest way to bring them nearer in judgment. *Having the same love.* Observe, the same love that we are required to express to others, others are bound to express to us. Christian love ought to be mutual love. Love, and you shall be loved. *Being of one accord, and of one mind;* not crossing and thwarting, or driving on separate interests, but unanimously agreeing in the great things of God and keeping the *unity of the Spirit* in other differences." (Matthew Henry)

"But even if my life is to be poured out like a drink offering to complete the sacrifice of your faithful service (that is, if I am to die for you), **I will rejoice, and I want to share my joy** with all of you. And you should **be happy about this and rejoice with me.**" Phil 2:17-18

P5. "Paul isn't being morbid here, asking the Philippians to take joy in something as depressing as his death; but he does ask the Philippians to see his death as something that will bring glory to God--a theme repeated from Philippians 1:20. Paul's life was going to be a sacrifice for Jesus Christ, either in life or in death; this was a source of gladness and joy for Paul, and he wants the Philippians to adopt the same attitude. Again, we come to the consistent theme of Philippians, *joy* - but it is a joy that is based not on circumstances (quite the opposite, really), but in the fact of a life totally committed to Jesus Christ." (David Guzik)

P6. The sacrifice of service mentioned by Paul is not a loss but an exchange for something much better. In this world sacrifice is often seen as a loss, but with God it is an exchange of something physical with something spiritual, a giving up of one thing to attain something much greater. Where sacrifice is seen as a loss it brings pain and stress, where sacrifice is seen as a gift it is received with great joy and happiness.

P7. Christians have nothing to lose, for they have nothing, all is God's. As stewards, they distribute assets according to God's will. The more they spend on themselves, the less they will have for the Master. The more they give to the Master, the more they have for themselves.

P8. "Unfortunately, many believers experience joy in much the same way as the world does. When circumstances are favorable, they are happy; but when circumstances are unfavorable, they are sad and sometimes resentful. The only things that bring them joy are those that promote their own interests and welfare. But when believers seek to do the Father's will and please Him, they view sacrifice for Him with joy." (MacArthur 193)

P9. Living in Christ is a pleasure. The greater the sacrificing of the world and of self, the greater is the joy. It is our concern with our selves that limits our joy, not the difficult circumstances. As we live by faith, we let go of our overactive ego and rely on God's riches to make us happy. Thus, we experience true and lasting joy.

5

The Joy of Caring

Philippians 2: 19-29

You cannot care personally for everyone. But you can find joy in caring for those around you, especially in times of difficulties and disasters. Your great joy is in giving.

A. Check the Quotation that Appeals to You the Most

__ "Things done well and with a care, exempt themselves from fear. "William Shakespeare

__ "It is amazing what you can accomplish if you do not care who gets the credit. "Harry S. Truman

B. Read and Apply the Joy of Caring

[19]If the Lord Jesus is willing, I hope to send Timothy to you soon. Then when he comes back, he can cheer me up by telling me how you are getting along. [20]I have no one else like Timothy, who genuinely cares about your welfare. [21]All the others care only for themselves and not for what matters to Jesus Christ.

Q20. I genuinely care about the welfare of

_____.

Q21. The things that matter to Jesus Christ are

_____.

[22]But you know how Timothy has proved himself. Like a son with his father, he has helped me in preaching the Good News. [23]I hope to send him to you just as soon as I find out what is going to happen to me here. [24]And I have confidence from the Lord that I myself will come to see you soon.

Q22. I have proved myself in giving the Good News in

_____.

Q24. I have helped _____ in giving the Good News.

[25]Meanwhile, I thought I should send Epaphroditus back to you. He is a true brother, a faithful worker, and a courageous soldier. And he was your messenger to help me in my need. [26]Now I am sending him home again, for he has been longing to see you, and he was very distressed that you heard he was ill. [27]And he surely was ill; in fact, he almost died. But God had mercy on him--and also on me, so that I would not have such unbearable sorrow.

Q25. I helped someone in their need when I

_____.

Q27. God spared me from unbearable sorrow when He

_____.

[28]So I am all the more anxious to send him back to you, for I know you will be glad to see him, and that will lighten all my cares. [29]Welcome him with Christian love and with great joy, and be sure to honor people like him. [30]For he risked his life for the work of Christ, and he was at the point of death while trying to do for me the things you couldn't do because you were far away.

Q29. I recently welcomed with Christian love and with great

joy _____.

D. Fit It

When I am ill or do not feel well (2:26,27)
- I take an inventory of my symptoms.
- I try to discover the cause of my illness or unwell feeling.
- I seek medical help when appropriate.
- I make sure I get enough fluids and rest.
- I am careful to pace myself.
- I reduce my optional activities when appropriate.
- I read my Bible and seek spiritual strength.

E. Consider That

Jane has a tendency to complain when she sees things out of order. There is usually someone to blame, and it surely is not Jane. That brings a negative tension. What steps can heal Jane's negativity?

F. Remember: "Let your light shine brightly: Hold tightly to the Word of Life" (Philippians 2:15,16).

G. Journal It

H. Explore it further

We will be glad to see him, and that will lighten all my cares. Welcome him with Christian love and **with great joy**, and be sure to honor people like him." Phil 2:28, 29

P1. The joy of the Philippians was Paul's joy too. A traveler returning from a Christian mission is to be welcomed back with great joy. By doing this, the joyous ones somehow share in his or her mission.

P2. Epaphroditus was sent by the Philippi church as their representative to assist Paul. Thus, his work was the work of the whole congregation, his joy upon returning was the joy of the whole church. Paul could write like this because he knew both the Lord and the Philippians. He could tell that the Philippians would react with joy. This in a way sets a pattern for returning missionaries. It is a time of great joy that the Lord saw fit to use one of the people to spread His message. Their safe return is a signal for celebrating.

P3. When people come and go, we often ignore their coming and going. We pay little attention to missionaries and others as they arrive back and thus we miss opportunities for celebration. Former friends return and we forget to respond to their return with joy. Paul knew that the Philippians, as good Christians would realize what a precious gift Epaphroditus was to Paul and to them. We are all gifts to each other. And gifts are to be received with thanks and joy.

P4. Paul's loss of Epaphroditus was the gain of the people of Philippi. Paul unselfishly gave him up so that he could return home and be with his family and church. That could have caused sadness to Paul. But he was so at one with the Philippians that he shared in their joy rather than wallow in his sadness.

P5. *That when you see him again you may rejoice* (v. 28), that you may yourselves see how well he has recovered, and what reason you have for the thankfulness and joy upon his account." He gave himself the pleasure of comforting them by the sight of so dear a friend. Paul recommends him to their esteem and affection: *"Receive him therefore in the Lord with all gladness, and hold such in reputation:* account such men valuable, who are zealous and faithful, and let them be highly loved and regarded. Show your joy and respect by all the expressions of hearty affection and good opinion." (Matthew Henry)

6

The Joy of Discarding Clutter

Philippians 3: 1-11

You cannot easily discard all useless things and ideas. But you can find joy in house cleaning and discarding clutter. You need only a few things to enjoy life.

A. Check the Quotation that Appeals to You the Most

__ "What a curious phenomenon it is that you can get men to die for the liberty of the world who will not make the little sacrifice that is needed to free themselves from their own individual bondage." Bruce Barton

__ "Civilization is being poisoned by its own waste products." William Ralph Inge, in *Wit and Wisdom of Dean Inge,* ed. James Marchant

B. Read and Apply what is Valued

[1]Whatever happens, dear brothers and sisters, may the Lord give you joy. I never get tired of telling you this. I am doing this for your own good.

Q1. Whatever happens, may the Lord give me joy in

_____.

[2]Watch out for those dogs, those wicked men and their evil deeds, those mutilators who say you must be circumcised to be saved. [3]For we who worship God in the Spirit are the only ones who are truly circumcised. We put no confidence in human effort. Instead, we boast about what Christ Jesus has done for us.

Q2. I watch out for wicked men like

_____.

[4]Yet I could have confidence in myself if anyone could. If others have reason for confidence in their own efforts, I have even more!

Q4. I used to have reason for confidence in my own efforts

such as _____.

[5]For I was circumcised when I was eight days old, having been born into a pure-blooded Jewish family that is a branch of the tribe of Benjamin. So I am a real Jew if there ever was one! What's more, I was a member of the Pharisees, who demand the strictest obedience to the Jewish law. [6]And zealous? Yes, in fact, I harshly persecuted the church. And I obeyed the Jewish law so carefully that I was never accused of any fault.

Q6. I was very zealous in

_____.

[7]I once thought all these things were so very important, but now I consider them worthless because of what Christ has done. [8]Yes, everything else is worthless when compared with the priceless gain of knowing Christ Jesus my Lord. I have discarded everything else, counting it all as garbage, so that I may have Christ [9]and become one with him. I no longer count on my own goodness or my ability to obey God's law, but I trust Christ to save me. For God's way of making us right with himself depends on faith.

Q8. The priceless gain of knowing Christ Jesus is to me

_____ .

Q8a. I have discarded _____ .

Q9. God's way of making me right with Him depends on

faith in _____ .

[10]As a result, I can really know Christ and experience the mighty power that raised him from the dead. I can learn what it means to suffer with him, sharing in his death, [11]so that, somehow, I can experience the resurrection from the dead!

Q10. I experience Christ's mighty power in

_____ .

C. Circle T for True or F for False and Give Reasons
- T F We can have joy under all circumstances.
- T F Over time, our appreciation of what is important changes.
- T F God's way of making us right with Him depends on our faith and on becoming good.

D. Fit It

I can really know Christ and experience God's mighty power (v 10) by:
- Thinking God's positive thoughts after him.
- Seeing God's humor in creation.
- Listening to uplifting music.
- Memorizing helpful scriptural passages.
- Cleaning out the clutter in my room, house, garage and life.

E. Consider That

Maria finds that much of her stress is connected with her cluttered house and limited resources. There is never enough space, money or time. So it seems strange to Maria that the way to joy is giving away some of these precious treasures. How would you help unclutter Maria's life?

F. Remember: "God's way of making us right with Himself depends on faith" (Philippians 3:9).

G. Journal it

H. Explore it further

> "Whatever happens, dear brothers and sisters, **may the Lord give you joy**. I never get tired of telling you this. I am doing this for your own good." Phil 3:1

"We are not commanded to rejoice in our circumstances, be they good or bad. No, we're to rejoice in the *Lord*. My circumstances may be bleak and brutal. But the Lord stands with me in those circumstances, and He will cause something good to come from them ultimately." (Jon Courson)

Joy is one of the fruits of the Spirit. It is a gift from God, not just a human emotion that we choose. Paul suggests here that the gift of joy may be given and received under all circumstances, not just favorable ones. Whatever happens, we can keep our face up and look with confidence to our Lord who will see us through the trials. We have no reason to doubt his supporting power. The Lord gives us the gift of joy in all circumstances; the question is whether we are able and capable to receive it.

"The joy of which Paul writes is not the same as happiness (a word related to the term "happenstance"), the feeling of exhilaration associated with favorable events. In fact, joy persists in the face of weakness, pain, suffering, even death. Biblical joy produces a deep confidence in the future that is based on trust in God's purpose and power. It results in the absence of any ultimate fear since the relationship on which it is based is eternal and unshakable... The result is a supernaturally produced emotion, the fruit of walking in the Spirit. Thus rejoicing marks the true believer" (MacArthur , 216).

7

The Joy of Focusing

Philippians 3: 12-21

You cannot do everything. But you can experience joy by focusing on one great mission. Funnel your energies that direction.

A. Check the Quotation that Appeals to You the Most

__ "To solve the problems of today, we must focus on tomorrow." Erik Nupponen

__ "Focus 90% of your time on solutions and only 10% of your time on problems. "Anthony J. D'Angelo, *The College Blue Book*

B. Read and Apply the Wisdom of Goal Setting

[12]I don't mean to say that I have already achieved these things or that I have already reached perfection! But I keep working toward that day when I will finally be all that Christ Jesus saved me for and wants me to be. [13]No, dear brothers and sisters, I am still not all I should be, but I am focusing all my energies on this one thing: Forgetting the past and looking forward to what lies ahead, [14]I strain to reach the end of the race and receive the prize for which God, through Christ Jesus, is calling us up to heaven.

Q13. I am focusing all my energies on

_____.

Q13a. I am forgetting the past, including

_____.

Q14. I want to reach the end of the race which is

_____.

[15]I hope all of you who are mature Christians will agree on these things. If you disagree on some point, I believe God will make it plain to you. [16]But we must be sure to obey the truth we have learned already.

Q16. To obey the truth I have learned already means for me

to _____.

[17]Dear brothers and sisters, pattern your lives after mine, and learn from those who follow our example. [18]For I have told you often before, and I say it again with tears in my eyes, that there are many whose conduct shows they are really enemies of the cross of Christ. [19]Their future is eternal destruction. Their god is their appetite, they brag about shameful things, and all they think about is this life here on earth.

Q17. I pattern my life after Paul's in

_____.

Q19. My god is my appetite when I

_____.

[20]But we are citizens of heaven, where the Lord Jesus Christ lives. And we are eagerly waiting for him to return as our Savior. [21]He will take these weak mortal bodies of ours and change them into glorious

bodies like his own, using the same mighty power that he will use to conquer everything, everywhere.

Q20. I eagerly wait for Christ to return as my Savior because

_____.

Q21. God will change our weak bodies into glorious bodies

like _____.

C. Circle T for True or F for False and Give Reasons
- T F On this earth I will never experience full and perfect joy amid the stress around me.
- T F I am an example to others, some of whom I do not even know.
- T F When Jesus returns, He will take our weak human bodies and improve them.

D. Fit It

I want to make sure that my god is not my appetite (v 19) by:
- Limiting my caloric intake to my caloric needs.
- Avoiding over-eating or under-eating.
- Refusing to be tempted by attractive unhealthy food.
- Refusing unnecessary drugs like alcohol and tobacco.
- Making God the Lord of all aspects of my life.

E. Consider It

June never had a clear vision where she was going. She just did what came along. Is there a larger meaning to her life? Should she have a focus in her life that she can call her life purpose? What is it?

F. Remember: I focus all my energies to reaching the end of the race and receiving the prize (Paraphrased Philippians 3:13,14).

G. Journal It

H. Explore it further

P1. 3 John 1:4
I could have no greater joy than to hear that my children live in the truth.

P2. Jude 1:24
And now, all glory to God, who is able to keep you from stumbling, and who will bring you into his glorious presence innocent of sin and with great joy.

8

The Joy of Experiencing Peace

Philippians 4: 1-9

You cannot constantly live in a sheltered rose-garden. But you can experience the joy of inner peace. God can set things right.

A. Check the Quotation that Appeals to You the Most

__ "Where ignorance is our master, there is no possibility of real peace." Dalai Lama

__ "Courage is the price that life exacts for granting peace." Amelia Earhart, *Courage*

B. Read and Apply the Lessons of Peace

[1] Dear brothers and sisters, I love you and long to see you, for you are my joy and the reward for my work. So please stay true to the Lord, my dear friends.

Q1. My joy and reward for my work is

_____ .

[2]And now I want to plead with those two women, Euodia and Syntyche. Please, because you belong to the Lord, settle your disagreement. [3]And I ask you, my true teammate, to help these

women, for they worked hard with me in telling others the Good News. And they worked with Clement and the rest of my co-workers, whose names are written in the Book of Life.

Q2. I did/will settle my disagreements with

_____.

[4]Always be full of joy in the Lord. I say it again--rejoice! [5]Let everyone see that you are considerate in all you do. Remember, the Lord is coming soon.

Q4. I am always full of joy in the Lord except when I

_____.

Q5. People can see that I am considerate in all when I

_____.

[6]Don't worry about anything; instead, pray about everything. Tell God what you need, and thank him for all he has done. [7]If you do this, you will experience God's peace, which is far more wonderful than the human mind can understand. His peace will guard your hearts and minds as you live in Christ Jesus.

Q6. I used to worry about

_____.

Q7. My way to experience God's peace is

_____.

[8]And now, dear brothers and sisters, let me say one more thing as I close this letter. Fix your thoughts on what is true, honorable and right. Think about things that are pure, lovely and admirable. Think about things that are excellent and worthy of praise. [9]Keep putting

into practice all you learned from me and heard from me and saw me doing, and the God of peace will be with you.

Q8. I fix my thoughts on

_____.

C. Circle T for True or F for False and Give Reasons
- T F Disagreements can be settled even if no side gives in or compromises.
- T F Settling disagreements can bring joy and minimize stress.
- T F I can always have joy in the Lord but not always have joy in the world.

D. Fit It

I settle my stress-producing disagreements (v 2) by:
- Solving small problems before they become big.
- Seeking some common ground.
- Forgiving.
- Focusing on solutions.
- Looking at my problems from God's perspective.

E. Consider That

Kim is frustrated with her past failure. Even though she attends church regularly, she is not at peace. How can she find that inner peace and make life joyous again?

F. Remember: "His peace will guard your hearts and minds as you live in Christ Jesus" (Philippians 4:7).

G. Journal It

H. Explore it further

> "Dear brothers and sisters, I love you and long to see you, for **you are my joy** and the reward for my work. So please stay true to the Lord, my dear friends." Phil 4:1

P1. "Paul found his joy in the people whom he loved." (MacArthur, 269) That was the immediate source of his joy. He did not look to humans for joy, he usually did not search for people who would love, bolster and encourage him. He looked for people that he could love in the Spirit of Christ. He always was a giver. We often look for joy in the wrong places. When we seek joy in our accomplishments, or our products, or our achievements, the emphasis is on the word "our", and then we realize we are selfish even when we do the best in our work.

P2. Whatever we do or say, there is always a "what" and a "how". We usually focus on the "what", on the content. We prepare what we will say at various occasions. We try to make things logical and plain; we organize and choose our words carefully. But in many situations, people do not really hear us and they are listening for the "how". Does the speaker understand me? Does he carry my burdens? Does he really care? Does he know me? The tone of voice is often all that comes through, the content is all filtered out.

P3. When Paul writes that the Philippians are his joy, there is much more than content at play. All along in the letter there is the "how" of it. The Philippians are Paul's joy in his prayers, in his memory, in his planning, in his feeling of satisfaction, and in his devotions. These words are not empty words but rather words full of deep meaning. The Philippians know that they are sincere expressions of Paul's deepest being.

P4. God gives us friends who to us are joy. So God's gift of joy is not given only as a supernatural feeling of trust in God, but also as a supportive certainty in relationships. Paul can tell the Philippians that they are his joy. The reason they are his joy is that Paul considers them part of his reward for his labors. They will be Paul's joy as long as they stay true to the Lord. This leaves open the door that in the future some of them could become his pain rather than his joy.

P5. Our human relationships are expressions of our divine relationships. If we do not connect well with the Lord, we cannot connect well with the people around us. The more we love the Lord, the more we will love our brothers and sisters. Love here means respect, giving them a place before we take our place. It means inviting fellow members to share in planning and decision-making.

"Always be full of joy in the Lord. I say it again--rejoice!" Phil 4:4

P6. This statement summarizes the joy message of this letter. The term "always" leaves no room for exceptions. Whatever the circumstances, good or bad, be full of joy. The term "full" also shows that there is not a degree of joy. We are not to enjoy some things a little and other things fully. As the Lord gives gifts without measure and limitation, so we should not ration and dole them out stingily. We can trust the Lord so fully that our cup runs over all the time. We never can rejoice halfheartedly.

P7. The passages that follow this text clearly outline the process of joy development. Paul reminds the Philippians that gentle people are joyous people. Joy takes away the hardness and harm associated with evil and sin and gives us a healing gentleness. We enjoy that healing because we trust our returning Lord and are not anxious for anything. We have nothing to worry about because Christ has forgiven our sins. For that we thank Him in prayer. Being thus close to Him gives us peace with God and peace of mind. God leads us into gentleness and prayer, and prayer leads us to peace. To keep that peace, a joy journal or a prayer list may often be helpful.

P8. "The only sure, reliable, unwavering, unchanging source of joy is God...Spiritual stability is directly related to how a person thinks about God...Knowledge of God is the key to rejoicing. Those who know the great truths about God find it easy to rejoice, those with little knowledge of Him find it difficult to rejoice." (MacArthur 274)

P9. "Happiness is caused by things that happen around me, and circumstances will mar it; but joy flows right on through trouble; joy flows on through the dark; joy flows in the night as well as in the day; joy flows all through persecution and opposition. It is an unceasing fountain bubbling up in the heart; a secret spring the world can't see and doesn't know anything about. The Lord gives his people perpetual joy when they walk in obedience to him." (Dwight L Moody,1837-1899)

9

The Joy of Getting Along

Philippians 4: 10-23

You cannot be buddy-buddy with all people. But you can find joy in getting along with people and refraining from harming them. Find the bridges to others that you can safely cross.

A. Check the Quotation that Appeals to You the Most

__ "A sense of humor is part of the art of leadership, of getting along with people, of getting things done." Dwight. D. Eisenhower (1890 - 1969)

__ "If all our misfortunes were laid in one common heap whence everyone must take an equal portion, most people would be content to take their own." Socrates

B. Read and Apply about Getting Along

[10]How grateful I am, and how I praise the Lord that you are concerned about me again. I know you have always been concerned for me, but for a while you didn't have the chance to help me. [11]Not that I was ever in need, for I have learned how to get along happily whether I have much or little. [12]I know how to live on almost nothing or with everything. I have learned the secret of living in every situation, whether it is with a full stomach or empty, with plenty or little.

Q10. I praise the Lord that I am concerned about

_____ .

Q11. I have learned how to get along happily with little or much, such as

_____ .

[13]For I can do everything with the help of Christ who gives me the strength I need. [14]But even so, you have done well to share with me in my present difficulty.

Q13. I can do everything with the help of Christ, including

_____ .

[15]As you know, you Philippians were the only ones who gave me financial help when I brought you the Good News and then traveled on from Macedonia. No other church did this. [16]Even when I was in Thessalonica you sent help more than once. [17]I don't say this because I want a gift from you. What I want is for you to receive a well-earned reward because of your kindness.

Q15. I give financial help to

_____ .

Q17. My well-earned reward for my kindness is

_____ .

[18]At the moment I have all I need--more than I need! I am generously supplied with the gifts you sent me with Epaphroditus. They are a sweet-smelling sacrifice that is acceptable to God and pleases him. [19]And this same God who takes care of me will supply all your needs from his glorious riches, which have been given to us in Christ Jesus. [20]Now glory be to God our Father forever and ever. Amen.

Q 19. God will supply all my needs by

_____ .

²¹Give my greetings to all the Christians there. The brothers who are with me here send you their greetings. ²²And all the other Christians send their greetings, too, especially those who work in Caesar's palace. ²³May the grace of the Lord Jesus Christ be with your spirit.

Q21. When I greet other Christians. I

_____ .

C. Circle T for True or F for False and Give Reasons
- T F One of the big lessons in life is how to get along happily on much or little.
- T F The secret of contentment is to be able to live happily with God's help in every situation.
- T F I have now all I need.

D. Fit It

I know how to live on almost nothing (v12) by:
- Reducing the clutter in my life.
- Focusing on priorities.
- Eating simply.
- Walking when possible.
- Eliminating unnecessary drugs.
- Being enriched by God's grace.

E. Consider That

Wanda's friends and neighbors are all better off than she is. Wanda considers herself poor. She feels that others are looking down on her. She is looking at others who have more than she has with a bit of jealousy. How can she obtain the contentment Paul had?

F. Remember: "I can do everything with the help of Christ who gives me the strength I need" (Philippians 4:13).

G. Journal It

H. Explore it further

P1. Philemon 1:7
I myself have gained much joy and comfort from your love, my brother, because your kindness has so often refreshed the hearts of God's people.

P2. Hebrews 1:9
You love what is right and hate what is wrong. Therefore God, your God, has anointed you, pouring out the oil of joy on you more than on anyone else."

10

The Joy of Overcoming Fear

Genesis 32:6-13, 22-28

You cannot easily give up all fears in your life. But you can find joy in trusting your fears to God who will see you through life's difficulties. You either live by fear or by faith.

A. Check the Quotation that Appeals to You the Most

___ "The way to develop self-confidence is to do the thing you fear and get a record of successful experiences behind you." William Jennings Bryan

___ "He that is down needs fear no fall, / He that is low no pride." John Bunyan, *The Pilgrim's Progress,* Pt. II, "Shepherd Boy's Song."

B. Read and Apply Lessons about Fear and Victory

"[6]The messengers returned with the news that Esau was on his way to meet Jacob--with an army of four hundred men! [7]Jacob was terrified [and distressed] at the news. He divided his household, along with the flocks and herds and camels, into two camps. [8]He thought, "If Esau attacks one group, perhaps the other can escape."

Q7. I was once terrified at the news that

_____ .

"[9]Then Jacob prayed, "O God of my grandfather Abraham and my father, Isaac--O LORD, you told me to return to my land and to my relatives, and you promised to treat me kindly. [10]I am not worthy of all the faithfulness and unfailing love you have shown to me, your servant. When I left home, I owned nothing except a walking stick, and now my household fills two camps!

Q10. I am not worthy of God's unfailing love, especially

_____.

[11]O LORD, please rescue me from my brother, Esau. I am afraid that he is coming to kill me, along with my wives and children. [12]But you promised to treat me kindly and to multiply my descendants until they become as numerous as the sands along the seashore--too many to count. [13]Jacob stayed where he was for the night and prepared a present for Esau."

Q11. I pray : Oh Lord, please rescue me from

_____.

Q12. God promised to treat me kindly when

_____.

[22]But during the night Jacob got up and sent his two wives, two concubines, and eleven sons across the Jabbok River. [23]After they were on the other side, he sent over all his possessions. [24]This left Jacob all alone in the camp, and a man came and wrestled with him until dawn.

Q24. I have wrested with God about

_____.

[25]When the man saw that he couldn't win the match, he struck Jacob's hip and knocked it out of joint at the socket. [26]Then the man said, "Let me go, for it is dawn." But Jacob panted, "I will not let you go unless you bless me."

Q26. I hung on to God and did not let go until He blessed me

when _____.

[27]"What is your name?" the man asked.
He replied, "Jacob."
[28]"Your name will no longer be Jacob," the man told him. "It is now Israel, because you have struggled with both God and men and have won."

Q28. I struggled with God and men for

_____.

C. Circle T for True or F for False and Give Reasons
- T F   Fear is often the mother of stress.
- T F   Joy relates to faith as stress relates to fear.
- T F   Prayer puts fear into perspective and thus removes stress.

D. Fit It

Deep breathing (Jacob panted, v26) is one of the best relaxing and fitness exercise:
- Expand your chest and increase the volume and ease of breathing.
- Breathe out all your fears, breathe in faith.
- Breathe with internal coordination.
- Improve your postural and breathing habits.

E. Consider That

Thomas has practiced stress management for some time now. He exercised, looked after his eating and has eliminated tobacco, alcohol and all unnecessary drugs from his life. But back of his mind there is a fear of an illness that could ruin his work-life and health. That fear seems to limit his joy and hold it in check, How would you help Thomas?

F. Remember: "I will not let you go until you bless me" (Genesis 32:26).

G. Journal It

H. Explore it further

P1. 1 Peter 1:8
You love him even though you have never seen him. Though you do not see him, you trust him; and even now you are happy with a glorious, inexpressible joy.

P2. 1 Peter 4:13
Instead, be very glad--because these trials will make you partners with Christ in his suffering, and afterward you will have the wonderful joy of sharing his glory when it is displayed to all the world.

P3. 1 John 1:4
We are writing these things so that our joy will be complete.

11

The Joy of Encouraging

Psalm 107:10-16, 2 Corinthians 7:4-7

You cannot be encouraged by all that happens around you. But you can encourage with joy all those that share your life mission. You can be the sunshine after a cloudy day.

A. Check the Quotation that Appeals to You the Most

__ "Seeds of faith are always within us; sometimes it takes a crisis to nourish and encourage their growth." Susan Taylor

__ "It is especially important to encourage unorthodox thinking when the situation is critical: At such moments every new word and fresh thought is more precious than gold. Indeed, people must not be deprived of the right to think their own thoughts." Boris Yeltsin

B. Read and Apply Encouragement for Prisoners of Stress

[10]Some sat in darkness and deepest gloom,
        miserable prisoners in chains.

    Q10. I sat in darkness and deepest gloom when I

_____.

[11] They rebelled against the words of God,
　　　　scorning the counsel of the Most High.

　　　　Q11. I rebelled against the words of God when I

_____.

[12] That is why he broke them with hard labor;
　　　　they fell, and no one helped them rise again.
[13] "LORD, help!" they cried in their trouble,
　　　　and he saved them from their distress.

　　　　Q13. The Lord saved me from my distress when I

_____.

[14] He led them from the darkness and deepest gloom;
　　　　he snapped their chains.
[15] Let them praise the LORD for his great love
　　　　and for all his wonderful deeds to them.
[16] For he broke down their prison gates of bronze;
　　　　he cut apart their bars of iron.

　　　　Q15. I praise the Lord for His great love by

_____.

2 Corinthians 7:4-7

[4] I have the highest confidence in you, and my pride in you is great. You have greatly encouraged me; you have made me happy despite all our troubles.

Q4. God has made me happy despite all my troubles when I

_____.

[5]When we arrived in Macedonia there was no rest for us. Outside there was conflict from every direction, and inside there was fear. [6]But God, who encourages those who are discouraged, encouraged us by the arrival of Titus. [7]His presence was a joy, but so was the news he brought of the encouragement he received from you. When he told me how much you were looking forward to my visit, and how sorry you were about what had happened, and how loyal your love is for me, I was filled with joy!

Q6. God encouraged me by the arrival of

_____.

Q7. "His presence was a joy" can be said about

_____.

C. Circle T for True or F for False and Give Reasons
- T F Sitting in darkness and deepest gloom is depressive.
- T F Spiritual depression is caused by rebellion against the Word of God.
- T F Prayer, God's love, and thanksgiving heal all spiritual distress.

D. Fit It

God snapped my stress-producing chains of:
- Debt.
- Overwork.
- Overweight.
- Clutter.
- Worries.
- Drug use. I have so much to encourage me.

E. Consider That

Bill was a great encourager. But there was one kind of people that Bill had a hard time encouraging. That was the people who put him down and in some small ways showed that they really did not respect him. What should Bill do?

F. Remember: "LORD, help!" they cried in their trouble, and he saved them from their distress (Psalm 107:13).

G. Journal It

H. Explore it further

P1. 1 Thessalonians 2:19
After all, what gives us hope and joy, and what is our proud reward and crown? It is you! Yes, you will bring us much joy as we stand together before our Lord Jesus when he comes back again

P2. 1 Thessalonians 3:6
Timothy has just returned, bringing the good news that your faith and love are as strong as ever. He reports that you remember our visit with joy and that you want to see us just as much as we want to see you.

P3. 2 Timothy 1:4
I long to see you again, for I remember your tears as we parted. And I will be filled with joy when we are together again.

12

The Joy of Forgiving

Matthew 18: 21-35

You cannot harbor evil against those that harm you and still love them. But you can forgive joyously even those who do not ask to be forgiven. Forgiveness is a great healer.

A. Check the Quotation that Appeals to You the Most

__The weak can never forgive. Forgiveness is the attribute of the strong. Mahatma Gandhi

__Mutual Forgiveness of each vice, / Such are the Gates of Paradise. William Blake, *The Gates of Paradise,* "Prologue"

B. Read and Apply concerning Forgiveness

[21]Then Peter came to him and asked, "Lord, how often should I forgive someone who sins against me? Seven times?"
[22]"No!" Jesus replied, "seventy times seven!

Q21. How often should I forgive so-and-so who sins against

me? _____.

²³"For this reason, the Kingdom of Heaven can be compared to a king who decided to bring his accounts up to date with servants who had borrowed money from him. ²⁴In the process, one of his debtors was brought in who owed him millions of dollars. ²⁵He couldn't pay, so the king ordered that he, his wife, his children, and everything he had be sold to pay the debt.

Q23. God brings his accounts up to date with us when

_____.

²⁶But the man fell down before the king and begged him, `Oh, sir, be patient with me, and I will pay it all.' ²⁷Then the king was filled with pity for him, and he released him and forgave his debt.

Q27. I was filled with pity and forgave

_____.

²⁸"But when the man left the king, he went to a fellow servant who owed him a few thousand dollars. He grabbed him by the throat and demanded instant payment. ²⁹His fellow servant fell down before him and begged for a little more time. `Be patient and I will pay it,' he pleaded. ³⁰But his creditor wouldn't wait. He had the man arrested and jailed until the debt could be paid in full.

Q26. I demanded instant payment of

_____.

³¹"When some of the other servants saw this, they were very upset. They went to the king and told him what had happened. ³²Then the king called in the man he had forgiven and said, `You evil servant! I forgave you that tremendous debt because you pleaded with me. ³³Shouldn't you have mercy on your fellow servant, just as I had mercy on you?' ³⁴Then the angry king sent the man to prison until he

had paid every penny.

Q32. God forgave me that tremendous debt of

_____.

Q33. Should not I have had mercy on my fellow servant

when he/she_____.

[35]"That's what my heavenly Father will do to you if you refuse to forgive your brothers and sisters in your heart."

Q35. My heavenly Father will refuse to forgive me if

_____.

C. Circle T for True or F for False and Give Reasons
- T F The forgiven are expected to forgive others.
- T F A forgiving attitude is usually upsetting and stressful.
- T F Forgiveness is both a physical and spiritual transaction.

D. Fit It

Forgiveness is one of the keys that brings joy into stressful lives. The five steps in granting the gift of forgiveness are:

A. Acknowledge the anger and hurt caused by the clearly identified specific offense(s).
B. Bar revenge and any thought of inflicting harm as repayment or punishment to the offender.
C. Consider the offender's perspective. Try to understand his/her attitude and behavior.
D. Decide to accept the hurt without unloading it on the offender. Passing it back and forth magnifies it.

E. Extend good will to the offender. That releases the offended from the offense.

E. Consider That

Joe had a hard time putting up with the people he worked with, especially his boss. But in spite of that, there was a good working atmosphere there. As Joe read Matthew 18, he wondered if that was, in part, due to a forgiving spirit that permeated the workplace. What do you think?

F. Remember: "The king was filled with pity…and forgave his debt" (Matthew 18:27).

G. Journal It

H. Explore it further

P1. "We forgive others, but often have a hart time forgiving ourselves. We do not have to let ourselves be victimized by others, and when we do, we can forgive ourselves. If we do not want to be victimized, we have to take responsibility for our actions. No one can offend us, unless we let them offend us. We can learn to protect ourselves." These were some of the discussion group comments by Sharon Perry on that topic.

P2. 2 Corinthians 8:2
Though they have been going through much trouble and hard times, their wonderful joy and deep poverty have overflowed in rich generosity.

P3. Galatians 5:22
But when the Holy Spirit controls our lives, he will produce this kind of fruit in us: love, joy, peace, patience, kindness, goodness, faithfulness, gentleness, and self-control.

13

The Joy of Enduring

---

2 Corinthians 6:3-10

You cannot be praised by everyone. But you can endure with joy all the negative things people throw at you. God helps you to cope with them.

A. Check the Quotation that Appeals to You the Most

__ "He that can't endure the bad, will not live to see the good." Jewish Proverb

__ "The manner in which one endures what must be endured is more important than the thing that must be endured." Dean Gooderham Acheson, quoted by Merle Miller in *Plain Speaking.*

B. Read and Apply Paul's Resources in Dealing with Stress

[3]We try to live in such a way that no one will be hindered from finding the Lord by the way we act, and so no one can find fault with our ministry. [4]In everything we do we try to show that we are true ministers of God. We patiently endure troubles and hardships and calamities of every kind.

Q3. Can I say, "No one can find fault with my ministry?"

_____.

Q4. I patiently endured troubles, hardships and calamities

when I _____.

[5]We have been beaten, been put in jail, faced angry mobs, worked to exhaustion, endured sleepless nights, and gone without food.

Q5. I have worked for the Lord to exhaustion when I

_____.

[6]We have proved ourselves by our purity, our understanding, our patience, our kindness, our sincere love, and the power of the Holy Spirit. [7]We have faithfully preached the truth. God's power has been working in us. We have righteousness as our weapon, both to attack and to defend ourselves.

Q6. We have proved ourselves by our

_____.

Q7. God's power has been working in us when we

_____.

[8]We serve God whether people honor us or despise us, whether they slander us or praise us. We are honest, but they call us impostors. [9]We are well known, but we are treated as unknown. We live close to

death, but here we are, still alive. We have been beaten within an inch of our lives. [10]Our hearts ache, but we always have joy. We are poor, but we give spiritual riches to others. We own nothing, and yet we have everything.

Q8. We served God when people despised us at

_____.

Q10. Our hearts ache, but we always have joy because

_____.

Q10a. We have everything, especially

_____.

C. Circle T for True or F for False and Give Reasons
- T F   Christians have to put up with stress.
- T F The Christian's weapon against stress and trouble is righteousness.
- T F   It is very difficult to experience joy amid high stress.

D. Fit It

We have proved ourselves (v6) by:
- Our purity of motives and priorities.
- Our understanding of joy.
- Our patience with institutions.
- Our kindness to difficult people.
- Our sincere love of the people around us.

- Our endurance under stress.
- The power of the Holy Spirit.

E. Consider This

Tom by now has accepted the fact that he will never be very rich or have the most prestigious job or family. He even has learned to resolve conflicts and solve the common problems that come his way. He is managing his stress rather well. He goes to church regularly and helps the poor. But the joy that this guide speaks of still eludes him. What is still missing?

F. Remember: "Our hearts ache, but we always have joy"
(2 Corinthians 6:10).

G. Journal It

H. Explore it further

P1. Colossians 1:11
We also pray that you will be strengthened with his glorious power so that you will have all the patience and endurance you need. May you be filled with joy.

P2. 1 Thessalonians 1:6
So you received the message with joy from the Holy Spirit in spite of the severe suffering it brought you. In this way, you imitated both us and the Lord.

P3. 1 Peter 1:6
So be truly glad! There is wonderful joy ahead, even though it is necessary for you to endure many trials for a while.

Part III

Discussion Guide for

The Healing of Stress

Just like Paul and the Philippians, you can experience joy amid stress. Study this part to gain deeper insights into joy and stress as you prepare for 13 more discussions.

Paul experienced combat stress. He faced death daily. There was no let up to his prison term, to the frustrations of not being able to make his physical position secure. In that environment and in spite of all, his spiritual life was sure. He trusted Christ to see him through it all. Thus he experienced the joy of salvation even in his prison cell.

Today in the army, combat stress is treated with what is called "three hots and a cot", namely three days of relaxing and sleep in a nice place with hot food, 24-hour counseling, and a real bed. Paul had none of these physical advantages, but he had supernatural help.

The word "joy" is used at least 13 times in the four chapters of Philippians, at times two or three times in the same sentence. Paul, who was a scholar and usually a serious writer, seldom dealt with emotions and feelings. But here in the letter to the Philippians, he wrote from a heart overflowing with gladness. He had worked in Philippi, he had befriended some of the people there, and these relationships were to him a source of deep satisfaction.

To fully understand Paul's emotional relationship with the Philippians, one must go back to Acts 16 where his first encounter with them is described.

Paul was guided by the Holy Spirit to the places where he preached. In Troas, Paul had a vision of a man from Macedonia pleading with him: "Come over to Macedonia to help us" (Acts 16:9). So Paul and Silas, his companion, immediately sailed from Troas to Samothrace, then to Neapolis, and from there to Philippi, "the foremost city of that part of Macedonia, a colony." (Acts 16:11, 12). Paul and Silas were thrilled to be thus lead by the Holy Spirit. They were not traveling to a place of their choosing, but the Holy Spirit was their personal guide. That was to them a source of great joy. They were partners with divine power.

We start with Paul's Event 1 in Philippi. There, Paul and Silas knew nobody and thus most likely stayed in an inn. On Sabbath they looked for some devoted Jews and found some worshippers by the riverside.

Among them was Lydia, a merchant of expensive cloth. She and her household soon became believers. Lydia invited Paul and Silas to her home.

Event 2 landed Paul and Silas in jail because they cast a demon out of a prophesying servant girl. The owner of the girl became most unhappy in losing his source of income and had them arrested. They sang and prayed aloud in prison and were freed by a miraculous earthquake. The result of this was another group of converts, the jailer and his whole family. Before they left the jailer's home, they all had a feast to celebrate the night baptism.

Event 3 was a later brief stopover by Paul to collect an offering for the poor on his way to Jerusalem. (Acts 20:1-3). The Philippians were liberal people and not only helped then, but also assisted Paul when he was in prison.

That brings us to Event 4 which deals with Epaphroditus, a believer from Philippi. He was sent to assist Paul in prison but himself got sick and nearly died. Paul is sending him back to Philippi with thanks and this letter to the Philippians. This is about all we know about the Christians in Philippi.

Continuous Joy

Continuos joy amid stressful circumstances seems like an impossible situation. Stress can be managed and often minimized, but it remains a fact of life. Difficulties and troubles bring stress. The difficulties and troubles of life are not going away nor are they decreasing. Stress management usually deals with reducing stress and coping with it.

Joy is one of the gateways to physical and mental healing. Many of the joys presented in this guide are connected with prayer. The joy of thanking includes the joy of thanking God in prayer. The joy of trusting includes the joy of trusting God in prayer. The same can be said for all the other joys described in this guide. Prayer links us to the source of joy, namely God. And God is the source of healing stress. Connected with God in prayer, we thus can have joy amid stress.

What then prompted Paul to write some very insightful statements on joy in his letter to the Philippians? The following section examines each of these statements.

In his letter to the Philippians, Paul describes some of the stressful aspects of his stay in Rome. The joy he expressed in his letter was not a sheltered experience in a rose garden. It was a joy in spite of his daily battle with Satan. The 13 discussions contain descriptions of some of these stresses.

Instructions for Discussions

Each of the 13 discussions is divided into three parts:

1. The scriptural passage consists of a number of texts that are framed. Each text is numbered. In the circle of participants, one person reads the first text, paraphrases it, comments on it, and leads out in a general discussion on it. Then the person to his or her right considers the next text in the same way, until all texts have been dealt with.

2. The questions are again marked Q1, Q2 etc. In the circle of participants, one person starts and leads out with Q1, then the person to the right of him or her takes Q2 and so on.

3. The comments in the following paragraphs are numbered P1, P2, etc. Again, in the circle, one person reads and leads out in the discussion of P1, and then the person to the right of him or her takes P2 and so on.

To conclude the discussion, the last person in the circle summarizes the discussion and leads in group prayer where all participants share their prayer concerns and are welcome to pray.

1

Healing for the Stress of Isolation

Philippians 1: 7, 13

Stress of Isolation

[7]It is right that I should feel as I do about all of you, for you have a very special place in my heart. We have shared together the blessings of God, both when I was in prison and when I was out, defending the truth and telling others the Good News. [13]Everyone around here knows why I am in prison. It is because I preached about Jesus Christ. All the soldiers who work for the leader of the country know why I am here. Philippians 1:7, 13

Q1. Who/What? _____.

Q2. Where/How? _____.

Q3. Prison means _____.

Q4. Good News means _____.

Q5. I grow by sharing _____.

Q6. I am here because _____.

P1. Prison is a stressful place. There is no freedom to move, to choose activities, to select books to read. Nearly all is prescribed. The emphasis is on security, the prisoner is not to walk away. In the days of Rome, there often was triple security. The prisoner was in chains, he was in stocks, and then he was behind locked doors. If he could throw off his chains, the stocks and the prison gate would still hold him in.

P2. The prisoner was fed and allowed to go to the bathroom. The arrangement for both was often very limited. Many prisoners got sick and died before they had their turn at the limited justice that existed in those days. In many cases, the guards were abusive and treated the prisoners roughly.

P3. It usually took some outside help to just survive in prison. For Paul, that help came from Timothy, Epaphroditus and most likely others Christians who lived in Rome. Thus his meals may have been supplemented with those brought by his friends. Paul could talk to his friends as they came to visit him.

P4. In those days they did not have visitor's rooms where prisoners and visitors could freely move around. Paul's visitors most likely were locked in with Paul. To Paul they were a source of great encouragement. He must have looked forward to their visits.

P5. At a previous occasion in a prison in Philippi, Paul and Silas had spent the night praying and singing. They had enjoyed worship even in the most difficult circumstances. In the Roman prison, Paul dictated a letter of joy. The guards could lock up his body, but not his spirit. With his spirit Paul kept connected to his Source of strength, the Holy Spirit. While his prison was stressful, he realized that God had a purpose in allowing him to be there so that he could live above that stress and thus to find his joy in his Lord.

P6. "He did not ignore or make light of his imprisonment, but it was incidental to his willing, joyous and immeasurable privileged status as a bondservant of Jesus Christ...Paul's chains were somewhat longer than a modern handcuff, about eighteen inches long. One end was attached to the prisoner's wrist, the other to the guard's." (MacArthur, 58, 60)

2

Healing the Stress of Rivalry

Philippians 1: 15-17

Stress of Rivalry

[15]Some are preaching out of jealousy and rivalry. But others preach about Christ with pure motives. [17]Those others do not have pure motives as they preach about Christ. They preach with selfish ambition, not sincerely, intending to make my chains more painful to me. Philippians 1: 15, 17

Q1. Who/What? _____.

Q2. Where/How? _____.

Q3. Rivalry means _____.

Q4. Pure motives means _____.

Q5. I grow by pure motives in _____.

Q6. I am sincere in _____.

P1. "Now this would be a stumbling-block and discouragement to some, that there were those who envied Paul's reputation in the churches, and the interest he had among the Christians, and endeavored to supplant and undermine him. They were secretly pleased when he was laid up in prison, that they might have the better opportunity to steal away the people's affections; and they laid themselves out the more in preaching, that they might gain to themselves the reputation they envied him: *Supposing to add affliction to my bonds.* They thought hereby to grieve his spirit, and make him afraid of losing his interest, uneasy under his confinement, and impatient for release. It is sad that there should be men who profess the gospel, especially who preach it, who are governed by such principles as these, who should preach Christ in spite to Paul, and to increase the affliction of his bonds. Let us not think it strange if in these later and more degenerate ages of the church there should be any such. However, there were others who were animated by Paul's sufferings to preach Christ the more vigorously." (Matthew Henry)

P2. As if Paul did not have enough trouble being locked up, one group of Roman Christians added to his difficulties. They were some Christians who preached Christ in order to show off their wisdom and skills. They would not cooperate with the other Christians but put themselves forward as the great preachers that were doing a greater work than others.

P3. It was not that they preached a different gospel. They were not part of the close fellowship of Christians that labored together for the advancement of the gospel. They had to do things their way. They had a spirit of jealously and rivalry, something very strange when we consider that Christians are all part of one body, one fellowship.

P4. It is possible to do the right thing with the wrong motives. These Christians were doing a good thing, they were preaching about Christ. But their hearts were not right, they did it for the wrong reasons. Paul preached Christ because Christ had called him to preach with the help of his fellow-believers. There was never a feeling of competition or rivalry. Sometimes Paul let one of the believers lead out, sometimes he led out, just as the Holy Spirit directed. Paul did not have to do everything; he made room for the ministry of Timothy, Silas, Barnabas, Mark and many more. There was no rivalry among them. I can imagine that Paul often was grateful when one of his other team members took over and had the spotlight and gave him time to pray and support.

P5. Paul was no doubt stressed by the rivalry, competition, hostility and conflict with his fellow Christians. But he was able to look beyond their motives to the result. And the result was that Christ was being preached. Paul stated that he will ignore the motives here and just rejoice about the preaching of the gospel. It takes a great man to do that. Paul was such a man.

3

Healing the Stress of Danger

Philippians 1: 21-23

Stress of Danger

[21]For to me, living is for Christ, and dying is even better. [22]Yet if I live, that means fruitful service for Christ. I really don't know which is better. [23]I'm torn between two desires: Sometimes I want to live, and sometimes I long to go and be with Christ. That would be far better for me. Philippians 1: 21-23

Q1. Who/What? _____.

Q2. Where/How? _____.

Q3. Dying means _____.

Q4. Fruitful service means _____.

Q5. I want to live because _____.

Q6. I am/will be ready to die when _____.

P1. "Paul's strait was not between living in this world and living in heaven; between these two there is no comparison: but his strait was between serving Christ in this world and enjoying him in another. Still it was Christ that his heart was upon: though, to advance the

92

interest of Christ and his church, he chose rather to tarry here, where he met with oppositions and difficulties, and to deny himself for awhile the satisfaction of his reward." (Matthew Henry)

P2. A prisoner in a Roman prison always stood in the shadow of death. Many died in prison so that it was a usual thing. No inquest was held, no funeral permitted. To the guards, it was one fewer prisoner to feed and a bit less crowding in a crowded prison.

P3. Paul in prison always stood at death's door. There was no assurance that he would see the next day, next month, or the next year, or freedom. It was customary for prisoners to prepare to die. In this, Paul was not an exemption. He was not ashamed to admit that the thoughts of his own death sometimes crowded his mind. In this letter he traced the flow of his thoughts on death. In so many ways the conditions in prison were so bad that it would have been a blessing to be able to escape through death. Especially since he knew that at death he would sleep for a while and be awakened by his Lord at the first resurrection. That was a pleasant thought.

P4. Paul knew that he was in the Roman prison for a purpose. As long as the Lord was willing to use him here on earth, he was willing to serve. The circumstances mattered little. To Paul service meant helping with joy. Paul's joy grew out of his deep faith that the Lord was taking care of him and leading him. So in much or little, Paul could face all stress, even the stress of death around him.

P5. Death to Paul was not the ultimate end or something bad; it was the beginning of a full fellowship with Jesus Christ. He had this fellowship here on earth and he enjoyed it. But he also knew that a fuller fellowship awaited him after death. So Paul felt that he could not choose between life and death, but left the timing up to God. That was his faith and his joy.

P6. If our bodies are for vanity, our homes for prestige, our inheritance for riches, and our friends for popularity, then we live for self. If our lives are for God's glory, our homes for hospitality, our inheritance for sharing, and our friends for mutual service, then we live for Christ.

If our bodies are for sin, our homes for ambition, our inheritance for self, our friends for gain, then dying is loss.

P7. *If our bodies become supernatural, our homes heavenly palaces, our lives never-ending joy, and our companion Jesus Christ, then dying is gain at the resurrection.* For me to live is Christ, to die is gain. John 14:1-3, Revelation 21:1-7 (These paragraphs in P6 and P7 were part of a funeral sermon presented by the author in Placerville, California)

4

Healing the Stress of Suffering

Stress of Suffering

[28]Don't be intimidated by your enemies. This will be a sign to them that they are going to be destroyed, but that you are going to be saved, even by God himself. [29]For you have been given not only the privilege of trusting in Christ but also the privilege of suffering for him. [30]We are in this fight together. You have seen me suffer for him in the past, and you know that I am still in the midst of this great struggle. Philippians 1:28-30

Q1. Who/What? _____.

Q2. Where/How? _____.

Q3. Suffering means _____.

Q4. Struggle means _____.

Q5. I grow by trusting _____.

Q6. I am in the midst of a struggle with _____.

P1. Paul saw suffering for Christ as a privilege. He could remind his friends that he had suffered plenty and had survived. For him, the struggle had not yet ended. This Paul accepted as a matter of faith. That was how God was leading him. Paul wanted nothing else but to be led by the Lord. If that meant suffering and struggles, so be it.

P2. From a physical and mental perspective, the suffering took its toll and was at times most stressful. But Paul was not living just on the physical and emotional plain. Paul was also living on a spiritual highland that the physical and mental could not touch. Thus he had the assurance that he was doing God's will, that God was taking care of him and would see him through to the end. That gave him joy.

P3. "Suffering for Christ's sake is not a burden but rather a high honor He graciously bestows on His faithful servants." (MacArthur 96)

P4. This puts a completely different value on suffering. Suffering may seem physically stressful but it may be spiritually joyful. Suffering for Christ is an honor, not a pain.

5

Healing the Stress of Pride

Philippians 2: 3-4, 7

Stress of Pride

[3]Don't be selfish; don't live to make a good impression on others. Be humble, thinking of others as better than yourself. [4]Don't think only about your own affairs, but be interested in others, too, and what they are doing. [7]He made himself nothing; he took the humble position of a slave and appeared in human form. Philippians 2:3-4, 7

Q1. Who/What? _____.

Q2. Where/How? _____.

Q3. Selfish means _____.

Q4. Humble means _____.

Q5. I grow in humility by _____.

Q6. I make myself nothing in _____.

P1. Much of our stress is connected with our selfishness and false pride. We compare ourselves to others and we become dissatisfied. We do not quite measure up. We think of the gifts that we lack and we become stressed.

P2. We start from the top and look down around us. We are rich and increased in goods and see life from that tree-top. We lament when we think we lose something and we rejoice when we think that we gain something. We forget that often the losing is gain and the gaining is loss. In this world, values are so mixed up that we cannot measure them by their placement. In the end, the first will become the last and the last the first.

P3. When we are able to let go of our importance, we take a lot of tension out of life. Paul not only talked about humility, he also practiced it. He reminded his readers that Christ is the ultimate example of humility. The Lord had and has all, but He took the form of a child and later a carpenter to live humbly among us. He put up with much, and so did Paul. By His grace, so can we.

P4. From a spiritual perspective, we are all beginners and kindergarten children. The Lord is our Teacher and Master. We have no claims to wisdom or righteousness. We have no claims to positions and privileges. What is coming to us is deserved. Like Paul, thank God for the blessings.

P5. It is hard to live with people who have an inflated self-image. They consider themselves always right and resent it when others do not agree with them. They see every compromise as a matter of principle and thus they do not compromise, even on methods of doing things.

P6. "Selfishness is a consuming and destructive sin...Even when not outwardly manifested, selfishness breeds anger, resentment, and jealousy... Selfish ambition is often clothed in pious rhetoric by those who are convinced of their own superior abilities in promoting the cause of God." (MacArthur, 110)

6

Healing the Stress of Complaining

Stress of Complaining

[14]In everything you do, stay away from complaining and arguing, [15]so that no one can speak a word of blame against you. You are to live clean, innocent lives as children of God in a dark world full of crooked and perverse people. Let your lives shine brightly before them. [16]Hold tightly to the word of life, so that when Christ returns, I will be proud that I did not lose the race and that my work was not useless.
[17]But even if my life is to be poured out like a drink offering to complete the sacrifice of your faithful service (that is, if I am to die for you), I will rejoice, and I want to share my joy with all of you.
Philippians 2:14-17

Q1. Who/What? _____.

Q2. Where/How? _____.

Q3. Complaining means _____.

Q4. Clean living means _____.

Q5. I shine brightly by _____.

Q6. I hold tightly to the Word of Life by _____.

P1. Paul had plenty to complain about. So do we. But Paul asks us to stay away from complaining and arguing. When we complain and argue, we strain and eventually break relationships. The most precious gifts we have are relationships. Once they are broken, they are hard to patch up again. In many cases, the break shows even after the passing of years.

P2. Paul most likely was tempted to complain. He was very human. When things were bad all around him, he looked up and selected the spiritual drive. There, from a perspective of heaven, he had nothing more to complain about. The problems of the earth seemed so strangely small. Paul felt so blessed that even in the most difficult situations he could find heavenly joy. Others around him may have complained and become bitter, but not Paul.

P3. Complaining and arguing result in blame. There is a lot of blame to go around, when people are not willing to accept any responsibility for their part. Soon they are in unity with this crooked and perverse people. All of that can be avoided by just refusing to complain. Paul took his problems to the Lord, not to his friends. He knew that his words of complaints would discourage them because they could not help. The Word of Life is never discouraging. Paul took his complaints to the Lord and his joys to his friends. Thus he was able to minister to them and keep his own head above water. For complaints and arguments harm the complainer more than the recipient of the complaint. Once a negative cloud is released, all becomes involved in that harmful mist.

P4. "Adam was the first complainer. Immediately after he disobeyed God, he blamed Eve for his sin, complaining to the Lord ... instead of blaming himself, he blamed God.... Every circumstance of life is to be accepted willingly and joyfully, without murmuring, complaint or disappointment, much less resentment. There should never be either emotional grumbling or intellectual disputing.... Paul gives three reasons why believers should stop complaining: for their own sakes, for the sake of the unsaved, and for the sake of pastors." (MacArthur 196,180, 181)

7

Healing the Stress of Sickness

Philippians 2: 26-27

Stress of Sickness

[26]Now I am sending him [Epaphroditus] home again, for he has been longing to see you, and he was very distressed that you heard he was ill. [27]And he surely was ill; in fact, he almost died. But God had mercy on him--and also on me, so that I would not have such unbearable sorrow. Philippians 2:26-27

Q1. Who/What? _____.

Q2. Where/How? _____.

Q3. Illness means _____.

Q4. Mercy means _____.

Q5. I grow by overcoming _____.

Q6. I am at times distressed by _____.

P1. Paul had on his hands a helper who was sick. Epaphroditus had come from Philippi to help and encourage Paul. It had not worked out that way. Epaphroditus had gotten sick in Rome and nearly died there. Paul was troubled by that, since he himself could do so little for his friend. That is not what Paul needed. But that is what Paul got. Paul no doubt prayed for his friend.

P2. The sickness of Epaphroditus was a serious one. It was most likely an infectious disease, because he caught it in Rome. He nearly died, Paul writes. All this happened because the Philippians were trying to help Paul. In some sense, Paul came close to being responsible for the near death of his friend Epaphroditus. Had Epaphroditus not come to Rome to help him, he most likely would have been well. He came to Rome and got sick there.

P3. Sickness is stressful for the sick and for all around them. All at once, the normal strength is gone and many things are very hard to do. The sick can no longer help, but themselves become a burden to those around them. Sometimes they get well seemingly without help; sometimes they get well with medication or treatment, at other times they die. Those around them feel so helpless to assist. That is how Paul felt.

P4. Paul was thankful that he was spared the sorrow of the death of Epaphroditus. He called it unbearable sorrow. He credits the Lord with saving Epaphroditus. Paul had prayed for his friend and God had heard his prayers. In the midst of stress, prayer was a way out.

P5. The word to denote "sick" in Greek really means "without strength." Epaphroditus was so sick that he was without strength to serve, even losing the strength to live. That created stress around Paul for he too was a person without physical strength and freedom. Paul found his strength and freedom in Christ.

P6. "Epaphroditus was sick when he was with Paul--Paul, the one whose sweatbands were used to bring healing to people; Paul, the one who laid his hands on people and they recovered; Paul, the one who was known for moving in the miraculous! Why didn't Paul heal Epaphroditus immediately?

P7. For the same reason he didn't heal Trophimus (II Timothy 4:20), or Timothy (I Timothy 5:23), or even himself (II Corinthians 12:7). Ultimately, everyone will be healed, for by Jesus' stripes, we are *all* healed (Isaiah 53:5). The only question is timing. When they ask for healing, some are healed immediately. Others, five years later.

Others, not until they get to heaven. Healing is connected with a person's spirituality or faith, but ultimately, it has everything to do with God's sovereignty.

P8. "Three times Paul prayed for deliverance, only to hear the Lord say, 'No, Paul. When you are weak, then My strength is manifested. My grace is sufficient for you,' (II Corinthians 12:9). Thus, I encourage those who are afflicted to follow Paul's model, to pray 3 times, 30 times, or 300 times —until they receive what they're asking for, or until they have a peace in their heart which says, 'This is what the Lord has for me, and I can embrace it.'" (Jon Courson)

8

Healing the Stress of Religiosity

Philippians 3:2-3

Stress of Conflicts

[2]Watch out for those dogs, those wicked men and their evil deeds, those mutilators who say you must be circumcised to be saved. [3]For we who worship God in the Spirit are the only ones who are truly circumcised. We put no confidence in human effort. Instead, we boast about what Christ Jesus has done for us. Philippians 3:2-3

Q1. Who/What? _____.

Q2. Where/How? _____.

Q3. Evil means _____.

Q4. Circumcised means _____.

Q5. I grow by putting confidence in _____.

Q6. I am saved by _____.

P1. One definition of religiosity is excessive, overdone or effected piety. The difficulty often centers on what is appropriate and what is overdone in the religious life. Paul seems to feel that any human effort for the purpose of salvation was excessive.

P2. Conflicts are states of disharmony. One side stands for one purpose, and another side for an opposing goal. Conflicts take time and effort to be worked out, and some are never resolved. Many conflicts end only with the removal of one party.

P3. Any conflict is stressful, but religious conflicts are especially stressful. They go to the very basis of what a person stands for. Paul stood for salvation by faith alone. Salvation is a free gift of God to those who trust Christ. Nothing they do or do not do buys salvation.

P4. Another source of potential stress for Paul was the false teaching of some Christians. They were saying that circumcision of males was a requirement for salvation. Paul was very upset by them; he called them evil dogs and mutilators. Their false teachings went against the fundamental truth about Christ. If people can earn salvation by anything they do, they would not need Christ. Salvation is not by faith and works, whatever the works may be. Most religions are based on works, on things people must do to appease an angry god. Christianity is different.

P5. Christians are often confused because it appears in Matthew 25 that people will be judged on whether they help others or not, and that seems to be works. Loving help is not work, it is part of God's gift of salvation. Love is a Fruit of the Spirit that God grows in His faithful followers. We cannot truly love without Christ's presence in our hearts.

P6. "Salvation is by grace alone through faith alone... No ritual – not circumcision, baptism, communion, or any other – can transform the heart. And only those with transformed hearts can please God." (MacArthur 218, 219)

9

Healing the Stress of Bad Memories

Philippians 3: 13-14

Stress of Bad Memories

[13]No, dear brothers and sisters, I am still not all I should be, but I am focusing all my energies on this one thing: Forgetting the past and looking forward to what lies ahead, [14]I strain to reach the end of the race and receive the prize for which God, through Christ Jesus, is calling us up to heaven. Philippians 3:13-14

Q1. Who/What? _____.

Q2. Where/How? _____.

Q3. Focusing means _____.

Q4. Prize means _____.

Q5. I grow by focusing _____.

Q6. I strain to reach the end of _____.

P1. "Some people are always looking back. They cannot get over what happened to them last year, five years ago, or twenty years ago. 'She hurt me.' 'He fired me.' 'That company misused me,' they say. Paul says just the opposite. 'This is what I do: I forget the stuff which is behind. And the same mind is to be in you.' The sin which we've committed in the past will condemn us to the place of paralysis. And the good stuff we've done by His grace will puff us up to the place of pride. Thus, our only option is to do what Paul did: forget the past. We must be those who say, 'I'm not going to dwell on that. I'm not going to be tripped up by that. I'm not going to glory in that. I'm not going to be confused about that. All of that is behind me. I'm moving on.'" (Jon Courson)

P2. Paul lived with the knowledge of his own unworthiness. He had not earned salvation. He was not perfect. The memories of his past evil were with him. Paul had stood by when Stephan was murdered. He had made many mistakes. Some of these were reminders that he continuously needed Christ's righteousness to see him through.

P3. Paul was in a race, on a journey. The race and journey were not yet finished. He was tired and worn, but he kept on going. He would not give up. He saw the goal before him and his faith that Christ would sustain him to the end did not falter. The forces that tried to slow him down were great, but the sustaining power of God was greater. He fully trusted that God would see him through to the very end, whatever that was.

P4. Paul did not look back on his failures. He was not discouraged by the present difficulties. Spiritually he lived in the future when he would be in the wonderful presence of Jesus Christ.

P5. "A runner who looks back risks being passed. Nor does a runner's performance in past races guarantee success or failure in present or future races. The past is not relevant; what matters is making the maximum effort in the present so as to sustain momentum in the future. Perfectionists and legalists look to their past achievement to validate their supposed spiritual status.... Believers cannot live on past victories nor should they be debilitated by the guilt of past sins." (MacArthur, 247)

10

Healing the Stress of Overeating

Stress of Overeating

[19]Their future is eternal destruction. Their god is their appetite, they brag about shameful things, and all they think about is this life here on earth. Philippians 3:19

Q1. Who/What? _____.

Q2. Where/How? _____.

Q3. Eternal destruction means _____.

Q4. Appetite means _____.

Q5. I grow by controlling _____.

Q6. I think about _____.

P1. Paul realized that most people live to eat and limit their thinking and planning to life here on earth. They lack spiritual depth; all they have is the physical. The physical will pass away; all that will be left is the spiritual. After His return, God will make a New Earth and a New Heaven, as described in Revelation 21 and 22, a new physical world for us. This earth is passing away. Putting your investments into this world is not safe.

P2. "'What's the key to life?' he said. 'Women!' So he gathered 1,000 concubines — the most beautiful women in the region — only to discover they weren't the answer.
'Partying — *that's* the key,' he decided. So he imported baboons and peacocks from Africa to entertain his guests, while he kept the wine flowing freely. But after partying for years, he found it empty.
'Power — that's what will satisfy a man,' he surmised. So he expanded the boundaries of his empire farther than those of any other nation of antiquity. But even then he felt unsatisfied.
He studied philosophy and science — and garnered so much gold that silver was rendered worthless in his kingdom. And yet he declared it all empty.
At last he said, 'Power, prosperity, fame, partying, women, wine, education are not the answer. The only key to life is to fear God.' But by then, Solomon's most productive years were lost, wasted because his god was his belly; his glorying was in his own name; he minded earthly things.
Beware of those who try to get you focused on this life, worried about this life, caught up in this life.
They're enemies of the Cross, for the Cross says, 'Forget about yourself. Look towards eternity. Live for heaven.'" (Jon Courson)

P3. Living only in physical reality is not enough. There is also a spiritual reality that many people deny. God lives in a dimension that is invisible to us. But He is there nevertheless. He lives in a spiritual dimension that is now accessible for us only by faith and prayer. After Christ's return, that reality will be fully open to us and we will be part of it.

P4. Overeating is stressful. Many people get their main joy of life by eating. Nothing satisfies like a good meal. Good meals add up. The extra weight stresses all body systems. This makes it harder to cope with hardships. For many, the way out seems to be more food. Paul could see that all around him. Some prison guards most likely were in that class. They added to the burdens of life by overeating and drug use.

11

Healing the Stress of Disagreements

Philippians 4: 2-3

Stress of Disagreements

[2]And now I want to plead with those two women, Euodia and
Syntyche. Please, because you belong to the Lord, settle your
disagreement. [3]And I ask you, my true teammate, to help these
women, for they worked hard with me in telling others the Good
News. And they worked with Clement and the rest of my co-workers,
whose names are written in the Book of Life. Philippians 4:2-3

Q1. Who/What? _____.

Q2. Where/How? _____.

Q3. Disagreement means _____.

Q4. Teammate means _____.

Q5. I grow by settling disagreements in _____.

Q6. I work with _____.

P1. Disagreements among people are one of the greatest common
sources of stress. Even among Paul's friends there was conflict. Paul
knew about the ongoing battle of two Philippi women, Euodia and
Syntyche. Disagreements can be settled. It seems that these

disagreements concerned ways of doing things, not fundamental differences of faith. Both worked equally for the Lord, and Paul does not take the side of one against the other. From Paul's perspective, the disagreement was a minor one, not one that could not been healed.

P2. Disagreements are solved when one or the other party gives in or when both parties compromise to form a new joint way of action. Disagreements continue when neither party gives in nor neither party compromises. Religious people often make everything a matter of principle, and they consider themselves right and everyone else wrong. Everything is not a matter of principle and equally important. In the long run, most things matter little and are soon forgotten.

P3. Love covers a multitude of sins. Love forgives even when the offender does not ask for forgiveness. Thus for a truly loving person, it is easy to forgive and give in to the other. It does not matter so much. It is all right not to get your way. It is all right to give in. The one who gives in does not lose anything, he gains a friend. To the true Christian, friendships are much more important than feeling that he or she is right. Christ is our righteousness, not what I do today and tomorrow.

P4. Disagreements often bring the worst out of people. The healing comes with forgiveness. We are all evil. None of us is perfect. Thus it is all right to overlook the selfishness and stubbornness of others.

P5. "The more isolated a believer is from other Christians, the more spiritually unstable he or she is likely to be...The church should be a place where people support each other, hold each other accountable, and care for each other... There was a great danger that the Philippians would become critical, bitter, vengeful, hostile, unforgiving and proud... Paul knew that if both got right with the Lord they would be right with each other." (MacArthur, 270, 271)

P6. "Biblical counseling is amazingly simple. To those enmeshed in interpersonal conflicts, we can be like Paul and say, 'Even if you're technically right in any given argument, you're spiritually wrong because the Lord wants you to be forgiving and gracious and merciful." (Jon Courson) A friend recently told me that she was "too blessed to be stressed." That summarizes this guide well.

12

Healing the Stress
of Inner Emptiness

Philippians 1: 9-11, 2:5-11

Philippians includes three great passages about who God is. Some may call them three main doctrines. Carmen Christi is a song that highlights Christ's humility and glory (Phil 2:5-11). The second passage points out the way of salvation (Discussion 13). And the third passage points forward to Christ's return (Discussion 13).

[9]I pray that your love for each other will overflow more and more, and that you will keep on growing in your knowledge and understanding. [10]For I want you to understand what really matters, so that you may live pure and blameless lives until Christ returns. [11]May you always be filled with the fruit of your salvation --those good things that are produced in your life by Jesus Christ--for this will bring much glory and praise to God. Philippians 1:9-11

Kenosic Passion: Carmen Christi (A hymn to Christ)

"[5]Your attitude should be the same that Christ Jesus had. [6]Though he was God, he did not demand and cling to his rights as God. [7]He made himself nothing; he took the humble position of a slave and appeared in human form. [8]And in human form he obediently humbled himself even further by dying a criminal's death on a cross.

112

[9]Because of this, God raised him up to the heights of heaven and gave him a name that is above every other name, [10]so that at the name of Jesus every knee will bow, in heaven and on earth and under the earth, [11]and every tongue will confess that Jesus Christ is Lord, to the glory of God the Father." Philippians 2:5-11

Q1. Who/What? _____.

Q2. Where/How? _____.

Q3. Humility means _____.

Q4. Lord means _____.

Q5. My attitude is that of _____.

Q6. I worship by _____.

The following pages give further Biblical passages relevant to the healing of the stress of inner emptiness through joy.

In summary, the New Testament Passages on Joy Amid Stress are:

P1. 2 Corinthians 8:2
Though they have been going through much trouble and hard times, their wonderful joy and deep poverty have overflowed in rich generosity.
Galatians 5:22
But when the Holy Spirit controls our lives, he will produce this kind of fruit in us: love, joy, peace, patience, kindness, goodness, faithfulness,
Colossians 1:11
We also pray that you will be strengthened with his glorious power so that you will have all the patience and endurance you need. May you be filled with joy.

P2. 1 Thessalonians 1:6
So you received the message with joy from the Holy Spirit in spite of

the severe suffering it brought you. In this way, you imitated both us and the Lord.

1 Thessalonians 2:19

After all, what gives us hope and joy, and what is our proud reward and crown? It is you! Yes, you will bring us much joy as we stand together before our Lord Jesus when he comes back again.

1 Thessalonians 3:6

Timothy has just returned, bringing the good news that your faith and love are as strong as ever. He reports that you remember our visit with joy and that you want to see us just as much as we want to see you.

P3. 2 Timothy 1:4

I long to see you again, for I remember your tears as we parted. And I will be filled with joy when we are together again.

Philemon 1:7

I myself have gained much joy and comfort from your love, my brother, because your kindness has so often refreshed the hearts of God's people.

Hebrews 1:9

You love what is right and hate what is wrong. Therefore God, your God, has anointed you, pouring out the oil of joy on you more than on anyone else.

P4. Hebrews 10:34

You suffered along with those who were thrown into jail. When all you owned was taken from you, you accepted it with joy. You knew you had better things waiting for you in eternity.

Hebrews 12:2

We do this by keeping our eyes on Jesus, on whom our faith depends from start to finish. He was willing to die a shameful death on the cross because of the joy he knew would be his afterward. Now he is seated in the place of highest honor beside God's throne in heaven.

James 1:2

Dear brothers and sisters, whenever trouble comes your way, let it be an opportunity for joy.

P5. 1 Peter 1:6

So be truly glad! There is wonderful joy ahead, even though it is necessary for you to endure many trials for a while.

1 Peter 1:8

You love him even though you have never seen him. Though you do not see him, you trust him; and even now you are happy with a glorious, inexpressible joy.
1 Peter 4:13
Instead, be very glad--because these trials will make you partners with Christ in his suffering, and afterward you will have the wonderful joy of sharing his glory when it is displayed to all the world.

P6. 1 John 1:4
We are writing these things so that our joy will be complete.
3 John 1:4
I could have no greater joy than to hear that my children live in the truth.
Jude 1:24
And now, all glory to God, who is able to keep you from stumbling, and who will bring you into his glorious presence innocent of sin and with great joy.

13

Healing the Stress of Joylessness

Philippians 3: 4-11, 17-21, 4:4-19

Making Us Right With God

[7]I once thought all these things were so very important, but now I consider them worthless because of what Christ has done. [8]Yes, everything else is worthless when compared with the priceless gain of knowing Christ Jesus my Lord. I have discarded everything else, counting it all as garbage, so that I may have Christ [9]and become one with him. I no longer count on my own goodness or my ability to obey God's law, but I trust Christ to save me. For God's way of making us right with himself depends on faith. [10]As a result, I can really know Christ and experience the mighty power that raised him from the dead. I can learn what it means to suffer with him, sharing in his death, [11]so that, somehow, I can experience the resurrection from the dead! Philippians 3:4-11

Q1. Who/What? _____.

Q2. Where/How? _____.

Q3. Worthless means _____.

Q4. Goodness means _____.

Q5. I grow by discarding _____.

Q6. I am learning what it means to _____.

P1. Wait for Christ's Return. [17]Dear brothers and sisters, pattern your lives after mine, and learn from those who follow our example. [18]For I have told you often before, and I say it again with tears in my eyes, that there are many whose conduct shows they are really enemies of the cross of Christ. [19]Their future is eternal destruction. Their god is their appetite, they brag about shameful things, and all they think about is this life here on earth. [20]But we are citizens of heaven, where the Lord Jesus Christ lives. And we are eagerly waiting for him to return as our Savior. [21]He will take these weak mortal bodies of ours and change them into glorious bodies like his own, using the same mighty power that he will use to conquer everything, everywhere. Philippians 3:17-21

P2. [4]Always be full of joy in the Lord. I say it again--rejoice! [5]Let everyone see that you are considerate in all you do. Remember, the Lord is coming soon. [6]Don't worry about anything; instead, pray about everything. Tell God what you need, and thank him for all he has done. [7]If you do this, you will experience God's peace, which is far more wonderful than the human mind can understand. His peace will guard your hearts and minds as you live in Christ Jesus.

P3. [8]And now, dear brothers and sisters, let me say one more thing as I close this letter. Fix your thoughts on what is true and honorable and right. Think about things that are pure and lovely and admirable. Think about things that are excellent and worthy of praise. [9]Keep putting into practice all you learned from me and heard from me and saw me doing, and the God of peace will be with you.

P4. [10]How grateful I am, and how I praise the Lord that you are concerned about me again. I know you have always been concerned for me, but for a while you didn't have the chance to help me. [11]Not that I was ever in need, for I have learned how to get along happily whether I have much or little. [12]I know how to live on almost nothing or with everything. I have learned the secret of living in every situation, whether it is with a full stomach or empty, with plenty or little. [13]For I can do everything with the help of Christ who gives me the strength I need. [14]But even so, you have done well to share with me in my present difficulty.

P5. [15]As you know, you Philippians were the only ones who gave me financial help when I brought you the Good News and then traveled on from Macedonia. No other church did this. [16]Even when I was in Thessalonica you sent help more than once. [17]I don't say this because I want a gift from you. What I want is for you to receive a well-earned reward because of your kindness.

P6. [18]At the moment I have all I need--more than I need! I am generously supplied with the gifts you sent me with Epaphroditus. They are a sweet-smelling sacrifice that is acceptable to God and pleases him. [19]And this same God who takes care of me will supply all your needs from his glorious riches, which have been given to us in Christ Jesus. Philippians 4:4-19

Guide to Additional Study

A pattern similar to that, which was used here for the study of *Joy Amid Stress* in the book of Philippians, can also be used for other topics and books in the Bible.

1. Select a Bible version that divides passages into longer paragraphs like the New Living Translation, the New King James Version, or the New International Version.
2. Use each paragraph as the unit for study.
3. Read the passage carefully and underline the key words that are central to the passage.
4. Define the keywords. If needed, look them up in a Bible dictionary or a regular dictionary.
5. Circle the verse number that contains the central message of the passage. At times, there may be more than one such verse. That verse or group of verses becomes the section to remember, and if possible memorize.
6. Ask yourself the questions Who? What? Where? and How? as it concerns the passage.
7. Apply the passage to your personal life.
8. Summarize what you have learned.

About the Author

Rudy Klimes was born in Sternberk, Moravia, Czech Republic. He was a citizen of Czechoslovakia by birth, a citizen of Germany by proclamation, and a citizen of Canada by naturalization. Since 1986, he has been a citizen of the United States.

As a child, he lived under the oppressive occupations of Hitler and Stalin. A survivor of the Holocaust and the Communist takeover of his home country, Rudy learned four languages before finally settling on English as his working language. Two ancient languages that were early in his curriculum were Latin and Greek. In Asia, he studied and used Malay, Korean and Japanese.

In 1948 he escaped the Iron Curtain with his father and brother and settled in Canada. Within three years, at the age of 19, he started teaching school, an occupation that has been his lifelong work.

After marrying a fellow teacher named Anna Homenchuk in 1954 in Vancouver, British Columbia, Rudy and Anna attended Walla Walla College in Walla Walla, Washington, where he earned a Bachelor's and Master's degree in Education. Later Rudy earned a PhD from Indiana University, a Doctorate in Ministry from McCormick Theological Seminary and a Master of Public Health from Johns Hopkins University. Rudy and Anna have been married over 50 years.

Rudy and Anna worked as missionaries in the Far East for 26 years. In South Korea and Japan, and later in Hong Kong, Rudy served as college president. (Most likely the only individual who worked in that capacity in the three chopstick cultures.) In 1969, the Minister of Education of Korea awarded him the Outstanding Service Award, and the President of Korea, the Order of Civil Merit, named the DongBaeg Medal.

While in Korea, three children were born into the Klimes family. Their names now are Anita Heidi Borrowdale, MD, Bonnie Klimes-Dougan, PhD, and Randall David Klimes, BSEng. In their tribe of 12 are four grandchildren, Justin, Torin, Tyler and Hudson.

Upon returning from Japan, Rudy and Anna taught at the Andrews University School of Graduate Studies. While living in Michigan, Anna received her Doctorate in Education at that University. Later they moved to Washington D.C. where Rudy served as Associate Director of the General Conference Health and Temperance Department. In 1986 Rudy and Anna went back to the Far East and Rudy became president of Hong Kong Samyuk College. In 1989 they returned to Seoul, Korea and there he established the Sahmyook University School of Lifelong Learning.

In 1994 Rudy and Anna returned to the USA. For the last ten years, they have periodically taught and assisted in the Ukraine. As adjunct professor, he teaches health online for Folsom Lake College. He serves as President of LearnWell Resources, a nonprofit organization that he helped establish in 1994. LearnWell Resources specializes in online continuing education in health and drug prevention and development assistance for the Ukraine. He also assists as Associate Pastor of a local church in making spiritual house calls and leading small groups, and as volunteer chaplain of a Placerville hospital.

Rudolf Klimes is a product of Europe (17 years), the Americas (30 years) and of Asia (26 years). He taught seminars and classes on five continents. He has been very blessed as a parent, husband, teacher, professor, health educator, administrator, author, pastor and missionary. His favorite greeting is "Blessings on us." Praise God who gives all these opportunities and makes him a pilgrim.

Bibliography

Courson, Jon, The Epistle to the Philippians, Online

Guzik, David, David Guzik Study Guide for Philippians, Online

Henry, Mathew, Matthew Henry Commentary on Philippians, Online

Holy Bible, New Living Translation: Wheaton, Illionois, Tyndale House Publishers, Inc., 1996. (Used by permission)

Jamieson, Robert, A. R. Fausset and David Brown *Commentary Critical and Explanatory on the Whole Bible* (1871) The Epistle of Paul the Apostle to the Philippians, *Commentary by* A. R. FAUSSETT, Online

MacArthur, John, Jr., The MacArthur New Testament Commentary, Philippians, Chicago: Moody Press, 2001

Peace, Richard; Coleman, Lyman; Sloan, Andrew; Tardiff, Cathy, Philippians, Joy under Stress, Littenton, Colorado, Serendipity House, 1996.

United States Department of Health and Human Services, www.mentalhealth.org

White, Ellen G., Sermons and Talks, Volume 2, Online

Note: All online sources may be reached via www.BibleD.org

Index

Donations and Book Requests

I would like to make a donation to LearnWell Resources for their Stress and Drug Abuse Prevention Services.

For every donation of $24, LearnWell Resources will ship you four copies of *Joy Amid Stress*. For discussion groups, we suggest donations of $100, for which LearnWell Resources will ship you 20 copies. That includes mailing and handling. This offer is good as long as the supplies last. Seventy percent of your donation will be tax deductible.

Make checks payable to LearnWell Resources

Send it to LearnWell Resources, Box 944, Camino CA 95709

Please complete and enclose the following information. Please print

Name_____

Address_____

City, State, Zip_____

Day Phone_____

Email Address_____

Donation of $_____

You may also order this book at www.amazon.com.

My Journal

My Journal

My Journal